PRACTICAL
Project
Management
FOR
AGILE
Nonprofits

PRACTICAL
Project
Management
FOR
AGILE
Nonprofits

APPROACHES AND TEMPLATES TO HELP YOU
MANAGE WITH LIMITED RESOURCES

KAREN R. J. WHITE

Introduction by Pamela Puleo

MAVEN HOUSE
PRESS

Published by Maven House Press, 316 W. Barnard St., West Chester, PA 19382; 610.883.7988; www.mavenhousepress.com.

Special discounts on bulk quantities of Maven House Press books are available to corporations, professional associations, and other organizations. For details contact the publisher.

While this publication is designed to provide accurate and authoritative information in regard to the subject matter covered, it is sold with the understanding that the publisher is not engaged in rendering legal, accounting, or other professional service. If legal advice or other expert assistance is required, the services of a competent professional person should be sought.
— From the Declaration of Principles jointly adopted by a Committee of the American Bar Association and a Committee of Publishers and Associations

Library of Congress Control Number: 2013934520

Paperback ISBN: 978-1-938548-00-0
ePUB ISBN: 978-1-938548-01-7
ePDF ISBN: 978-1-938548-04-8

Printed in the United States of America.

10 9 8 7 6 5 4 3 2 1

CONTENTS

LIST OF FIGURES

ACKNOWLEDGEMENTS

This book would not have been completed without the support of Jim Pennypacker, a wonderful editor, publisher, and friend. His gentle encouragement, especially when "writer's block" struck, was always appreciated!

I also want to acknowledge the numerous friends and associates who shared with me their experiences in supporting nonprofit organizations. It is their labors that initially encouraged me to write this book. In particular, I would like to thank Kerstin, Lori, Kelly, Jessica, Bethany, Pamela, John, and Ken; you never seemed to mind when I needed confirmation.

Finally, I would like to dedicate this book to all those volunteers and staff members out there supporting the nonprofit organizations that make our society so much better for all of us. Your efforts are indeed noticed by those you serve; I hope this book makes those efforts a bit easier to perform.

— Karen R.J. White, MSc, PMP, PMI Fellow
Weare, New Hampshire

INTRODUCTION

Applied Agility
Practical Project Management for Agile Nonprofits

Pamela Puleo, FAHP, CFRE
Vice President for Community Affairs
Concord Hospital, New Hampshire

Gone are the days when nonprofits were judged simply by their good works and the worthiness of their causes. Gone are the days when volunteers were plenty and fundraising was a community-based endeavor. It's a brave new world for nonprofits, a world where transparency, efficiency, and sound business practices must replace the benevolent approach, which characterized charitable operations of the past.

The expectations placed on today's nonprofit organizations continue to grow — expectations for increased productivity amidst diminishing resources, expectations for expanded programming to meet community needs, and expectations from donors who want to be assured that their investments are sound. A nonprofit's ability to meet demands, respond to expectations, and achieve goals may well depend upon its view of the future. Looking to the new possibilities along the horizon instead of focusing on the landscape in the rearview mirror may mean the difference between success and failure. And that's where *Practical Project Management for Agile Nonprofits* comes in. For the nonprofit to function and compete in the future, attention to applying project management practices and creating new mechanisms to attract and work with volunteers will be required.

xi

The world of the nonprofit executive is a busy place. Rushing from one event to another, moving from campaign to campaign, and working to fill service and program gaps to meet constituents' growing needs can leave the professional and his or her results fragmented. The reality that many nonprofits work through volunteers — rare commodities today — to achieve their goals makes it clear that it's time to employ new skills to fulfill the vital and necessary missions of our third-sector organizations.

The concepts presented in this book have been proven effective in the for-profit sector, which applies various project management tactics daily to manage operations and achieve key business objectives. These same concepts, applied to the work of nonprofits, can help organizations become more organized, productive, and successful, utilizing resources to their utmost potential. For example, all fundraisers are project managers. Direct mail, special events, capital campaigns — these are all projects unto themselves. The fundraiser's ability to apply and utilize project management techniques will improve effectiveness and outcomes. Simply applying a consistent approach to a project using a work breakdown structure could alone yield tremendous benefit by organizing the work elements into small, manageable activities. The addition of project milestones assures that the initiative is moving along a stated timeline toward a successful conclusion. While busy professionals might argue that they can't afford the time it takes to create work breakdown structures for all of their key activities, in fact they can't afford not to. Not only does this approach ensure that all aspects of an initiative are well-planned for, it assures continuity of practice should a leader — staff or volunteer — step down from their role, a hazard faced all too often in the nonprofit world.

Virtually every nonprofit relies in some measure on a volunteer workforce to support its activities. From board members to envelope stuffers and everything in between, qualified and committed volunteers are often the nonprofit's greatest assets. Yet relying on volunteers to shoulder the bulk of the organization's responsibilities in today's society could be a recipe for disaster. The volunteer landscape has changed dramatically over the past twenty-five years as traditional family roles have evolved and the millennium generation has come of age. The nonprofit that hasn't adjusted its approach to attracting and engaging a new crop of would-be volunteers may find that it doesn't have the human capital needed to fulfill its mission. Rather than longing for the good old days and bemoaning the loss, savvy nonprofits are adapting their organization's volunteer roles — and the way they recruit for those roles — to respond to a new generation of volunteer prospects. This new generation will seek out meaningful work on their own terms and expect the use of technology to drive communications and successful business practices to support their work. If nonprofits are fortunate enough to attract the attention of these "new volunteers," organizations will need to remain attentive to meeting their expectations, motivations and unique needs.

From organizational missions and strategic priorities to critical initiatives and key activities, the alignment of resources with project processes is vital to successful outcomes. There are a lot of moving parts, and project portfolio management enables nonprofits to effectively manage all the moving parts while building flexibility into the overall plan.

Both volunteers and funders expect successful outcomes — outcomes that represent measurable improvement and effective use of resources. Both constituent groups want to know that their investments of time and money are being put to best use and that the nonprofit that they share their most precious resources with is both productive and successful. As Ms. White outlines in her book, project management tools, including project portfolio management, will assure a nimble organization, one that is able to address the needs of today while preparing for the future.

PART ONE

Why Now?

1

Global Economic Impacts
on Your Nonprofit

Your nonprofit is challenged daily to be efficient and effective with the monies provided by donors. And industry studies indicate that overhead costs in nonprofits typically range between 10 percent and 20 percent of the organization's available funding. Wouldn't it be marvelous if some of those scarce dollars could be applied instead to programs supporting your nonprofit's mission?

Applying the knowledge and practices of the project management profession appropriately can help you meet that goal. A study conducted by the Center for Business Practices (2006) shows that organizations that acquire this knowledge and apply these practices typically see a 20 percent or greater increase in productivity, customer satisfaction, and employee satisfaction — leading to an increase in overall organizational performance. This book is designed to help you realize those benefits.

The Toll of the Current Economy

Nonprofits account for a huge segment of the overall global economy, which means that as the global economy expands or shrinks, so

3

ECONOMIC IMPACTS OF NONPROFITS

- An estimated 2.3 million nonprofit organizations operate in the United States.
- The nonprofit sector contributed $804.8 billion to the U.S. economy in 2010, making up 5.5 percent of the country's gross domestic product.
- In 2010, public charities, the largest component of the nonprofit sector, reported $1.51 trillion in revenue, $1.45 trillion in expenses, and $2.71 trillion in assets.
- In 2011, private charitable contributions, which include giving to public charities and religious congregations, totaled $298.42 billion.
- In 2011, 26.8 percent of adults in the United States volunteered with an organization. Volunteers contributed 15.2 billion hours, worth an estimated $295.2 billion.

Figure 1.1. Nonprofits are a large segment of the U.S. economy (Urban Institute (2012).

does the nonprofit segment. This global impact affects the amount of money as well as the number of volunteers available to nonprofits. And the current global economy is shrinking.

Unfortunately, the news we hear every day, whether local, national, or global, is the same: the ability of governments to sustain long-standing social programs is dwindling. Local, volunteer-based nonprofits ranging from churches and schools to hospitals and charitable organizations are being asked to provide the safety net that a society needs.

But these organizations, like yours, are being challenged by the economy. The demand to find new sources of revenue and new ways of improving your nonprofit's performance is increasing. Grants from governments and private foundations are harder and harder to obtain, and if you receive one it's probably a smaller amount than in the past. Likewise, long-standing individual and local business donors are struggling to contribute at the same level they did in the past, a reflection of their own economic struggles. Pledges made five or ten years ago are harder to fulfill, leaving large gaps in your nonprofit's budget.

4

Recent research on nonprofits by GuideStar (McLean & Brouwer, 2012) reveals that, for more than three-quarters of the organizations surveyed, gifts from individuals are smaller and fewer individuals are giving. And the primary way most of these nonprofits are planning to deal with the revenue shortfall is by reducing program activites and services.

What Does It All Mean?

As the global economy struggles to recover, local needs are making it even more crucial than before that the money nonprofits raise is distributed back to society via mission-supporting activities and not consumed by staff doing work that volunteers could do.

Your nonprofit has probably always operated on a tight budget, but now it's even tighter. You need to acknowledge that economic pressures are here to stay, so you need to be more strategic in how you approach fundraising and how you allocate funds to meet your organization's objectives. One way to do that is to learn how to apply just enough project management to assist in your decision making as you face continuing economic pressures.

2

The Changing Nature of Volunteerism

Many leaders in today's nonprofits came of age in the 1950s and 1960s. These were the decades of the single-income household, a sense of community, and a value structure that was shaped by the shared experiences of World War II and the Korean conflict. During these years women in particular were encouraged to participate in community groups and activities, such as the PTA, Girl Scouts, or working in their local church's thrift shop. Men were expected to contribute to their local community by participating in service and fraternal organizations such as the Kiwanis, Masons, and Rotary clubs. Local businesses viewed it as a good investment in their local community to support participation in these organizations. It was not uncommon to find a local fundraiser for the community hospital being planned and executed by a committee of volunteers consisting of the wives of a bank director, hardware store owner, practicing physician, and the local newspaper editor. And the men were all too happy to serve on the boards of directors of community institutions.

We saw a shift in this approach to volunteerism in the 1980s and 1990s. Changes in the economy and growing financial de-

THE DISAPPEARING VOLUNTEER

Figure 2.1. The hours of work required by employers have increased, especially in the past ten years, leaving less time for employees to commit to volunteer activities. At the same time, cuts in funding mean that nonprofits are relying more and more on volunteers to carry out their missions.

mands on businesses affected the ability of would-be community participants to volunteer within the local community. One significant factor that aggravated the situation, and which continues to have a major role, is the nationalization and even globalization of what used to be local industries. Through consolidations, mergers, and bankruptcies many local businesses ceased to exist. Most banks are now subsidiaries of national banks that don't have a close relationship to the local community. The philanthropic activities of the big-box stores that have replaced Main Street stores are often dictated by the policies of some remote corporations that have few or no ties to the local community.

Compounding the challenge to volunteerism during these decades was the emergence and standardization of the multiple-income family. The adults within a family unit plus any teenage members of the family unit are most likely committed to one or more employers. The hours of work required by the employer have increased, especially in the past ten years, leaving less time for the employee to commit to volunteer activities.

Additionally, the past several decades have seen an increase in mobility as families relocate to maintain employment. Or they might have chosen to commute from their residential community to employment in some other town. Many families no longer identify with a particular local community. Rather they identify with a more global community, perhaps a virtual community.

Recent years have also seen an explosion of social media tools, tools that permit interaction between individuals without any face-to-face or even voice-to-voice communication. Users of these tools, primarily recent college graduates and younger people, have embraced the technology almost to the exclusion of interpersonal relationships. They don't need to physically meet, greet, and converse with someone to feel part of a community. They're just as likely to feel like a member of a virtual community as they are their local neighborhood.

Changes in Volunteerism

We are now seeing the impacts of these trends on organizations that rely on volunteers. The generation entering the workforce today understands "community" to be "a virtual global community." They are more likely to embrace volunteerism in support of a global cause rather than a local issue. For instance, in a recent conversation with several 2010 college graduates, we discussed their options for community service. They were much more animated in their responses to concerns about global hunger than they were to the challenges of the local food bank. One of the graduates stated that her ability to raise money locally was limited because her social network was distributed around the globe. She wasn't constrained in her friendships by geography.

This heightened sense of being part of a global community also means that there's an awareness of global problems that need to be solved. These big problems attract the media and celebrities, so potential volunteers naturally gravitate to these causes.

Society, especially in the larger metropolitan areas, unfortunately seems to have lost an appreciation of those values honed in the previous decades. Corporations' focus on the bottom line has precluded any emphasis on volunteerism as a desirable corporate trait. Certainly there are large corporations that will support causes that are aligned with their corporate objectives, such as environmental matters. They tend to show their participation at the national level, however, not at the local community level where significant needs exist.

How Should You Respond to the Changes? Make Sure Your Nonprofit is Agile

So how must your nonprofit respond to this changing nature of volunteerism in order to insure that it has both the money and the volunteers needed to meet its objectives? It needs to become an agile nonprofit. But what sets an agile nonprofit apart from the rest?

Agile nonprofits acknowledge this evolution in volunteerism and address it. Leaders in agile nonprofits start with a review of the organization's strategic objectives. These objectives help agile nonprofits identify entities within their communities that might have similar objectives — organizations whose missions are aligned. For instance, employees at a pet supply store might have an interest in volunteering for the local animal rescue organization; employees at a grocery store might be interested in supporting a food drive for the local food bank. Requests for volunteer support and sponsorship are made to these entities. Just as a case statement is formulated for any appeal or campaign, agile nonprofits develop case statements for volunteer appeals. And those statements address the question that the prospective volunteer will be sure to ask, "What's in it for me."

Agile nonprofits also determine how to embrace the new generation. They review their fundraising and volunteer management techniques to ensure that they include approaches to which this new generation will respond. These approaches include leveraging Facebook, virtual meetings, and other forms of social

AGILE NONPROFITS ADDRESS THE NEW VOLUNTEERISM

Agile nonprofits:

- Identify organizations that strategically align with them and solicit volunteer support from them

- Develop volunteer appeals that make it clear to the prospective volunteer what's in it for them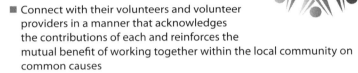

- Understand how to embrace the new generation, leveraging Facebook, virtual meetings, and other forms of social media

- Connect with their volunteers and volunteer providers in a manner that acknowledges the contributions of each and reinforces the mutual benefit of working together within the local community on common causes

- Have well-performing volunteer recognition programs that address the needs of volunteers, whether those needs are for public recognition, professional development, increased responsibility, or networking access

- Embrace business practices that enable the best use of available volunteers

Figure 2.2. How agile nonprofits address the changes in today's volunteerism.

media to assist in fundraising and in engaging their volunteers. Agile nonprofits minimize face-to-face meetings, lengthy written reports, and other tools viewed as bureaucratic.

Agile nonprofits connect with their volunteers and volunteer providers in a manner that recognizes and acknowledges the contributions of each and reinforces the mutual benefit of working together within the community on common causes. Agile nonprofits have well-performing volunteer recognition programs that include a means by which the needs of the volunteers are known and addressed, whether those needs are for public recognition, professional development, increased responsibility, networking access, or other considerations.

Summary

Agile nonprofits adopt and embrace those business practices that enable the best use of available volunteers. The full implementation of project management practices supports that goal. Knowing what positions on what project teams or committees are best suited for a particular volunteer, knowing what that particular volunteer values and is skilled in, and knowing the importance of that project relative to the organization's strategic objectives is crucial to being able to maximize the benefits of that limited resource: an hour of volunteer time.

So ... is your nonprofit an agile nonprofit? If your answer is no, or if you're not sure, read on to learn how you can help make your nonprofit agile.

3

Your Nonprofit in a Shrinking World

The world is shrinking, led by advances in communications, rapidly falling transportation costs, and sharply rising trade flows. This rapid globalization has a huge impact on our local economies — offshoring of manufacturing jobs, immigration considerations, and increased health concerns related to international travel. The shrinking world has a huge impact on our philanthropic efforts as well. Global disasters, especially those covered by the evening news, use multi-media to bring a heightened awareness of the events into our community. The resulting impact means that smaller, local events are often lost in the noise.

Consider the large benefit concerts given in response to Hurricane Sandy. There was an outpouring of

THE WORLD IS SHRINKING

Figure 3.1. Nonprofits need to be aware of the reach of their organizations.

support for Hurricane Sandy victims, but a significant apartment fire in a large city evoked minimal response. Some of the Hurricane Sandy response is related to the millennial generation's awareness of the global nature of their community and wanting to be part of something big. Another factor in the response is the multimedia blitz associated with the Hurricane Sandy disaster and the minimal coverage given to the apartment fire. An agile nonprofit seeking to obtain support for the local disaster could have initiated a local Twitter campaign to direct attention locally.

In this shrinking world you need to be aware of the reach of your organization — are you truly a local, community-based nonprofit relying totally on volunteers and staff who live nearby? Or is your community no longer geographically local — because of the transient nature of today's population or the ease of reaching people nationally or even globally? Consider the annual migration to Florida, the movement of students on college campuses, and the travels of people searching for employment. Today's society is much more mobile, more transient than in the recent past. We summer in cold regions, winter in warm regions. We attend college at a distance, returning home for holiday seasons, and then obtain employment in yet some other region. As you consider your various projects, how you find volunteers and staff to work on them, and how they communicate about the project, you need to think about your global constituency. It might be that the best sponsor for your project, an influential stakeholder, is someone who cannot physically attend monthly project team meetings but who might be able to participate by teleconference or online (say via a Skype session). If so, are you prepared to support that sponsor? Or is your volunteer pool constrained by geography?

In addition to reaching beyond your geographic boundaries for donors, you should consider reaching beyond those borders for volunteers. Recently I had a positive experience as a volunteer serving on an American Cancer Society Relay For Life committee. We had determined that we needed to broaden the awareness of the event to increase overall participation. In particular, we needed to reach communities surrounding our town, communities that were not in a position to host their own relay. To accomplish this goal we recruited volunteers from businesses and churches in those outlying communities, inviting them to join the committee or to support the relay events as a "day of" volunteer. Had there been committee members unable to attend the meetings physically, we were prepared to do a teleconference with them. We enhanced our ability to conduct marketing and to solicit sponsorships in those communities by having committee members who could do a "local ask." This in turn increased participation in the relay from those outlying communities, increasing participation in the event and thus an increase in funds raised. When considering a project, don't let geographical boundaries impose artificial limits on your volunteer pool.

PART TWO

Project Management
in Your Nonprofit

4

Nonprofit Projects

As the preceding chapters have demonstrated, you're working in a changing nonprofit culture and economy. Additionally, you're being asked more and more frequently to do more with the same or even fewer resources — be it staff, volunteers, equipment, or budget. You're also being asked to change directions midstream in response to unanticipated events. Applying project management approaches will enable you to be responsive to these demands in a calm and effective manner, whether you're a nonprofit director, a fundraising and development director, or a project manager. Project management and its various practices will support your organization's ability to "leverage the moment" — to be positioned to effectively deal with changing demands.

What is a Project?

The day-to-day management of your nonprofit (processing donations, acknowledging gifts, the handling of correspondence, doing bank deposits) comprises operational tasks required to keep your organization running. Projects, on the other hand, are focused on

TYPICAL NONPROFIT PROJECTS

- Special events: conferences, fundraising dinners, races, health screenings, art shows, etc.
- Capital campaigns
- Volunteer recruitment campaigns
- Building or upgrading a website
- Creating an annual report or a research report
- Direct mail campaigns
- Developing an education program
- Building a new facility or moving to a new facility
- Writing a grant proposal

Figure 4.1. Examples of some typical nonprofit projects.

meeting a specific goal, such as raising funds for a specific purpose, recognizing a certain group of benefactors, or holding an event. They each have a unique start and completion date and require some level of staff and/or volunteer effort.

The Project Management Institute (2013) defines a project as "a temporary endeavor undertaken to create a unique product, service, or result." When you think about the types of activities in which your nonprofit engages, you will realize that many of them are projects. Special events, appeals, and fundraising drives all meet this definition. Even a capital fund campaign can be considered a series of related projects with a common goal (known as a program). Figure 4.1 lists typical nonprofit projects.

What is a Project Manager?

When you embrace project management, you establish a focus on using project teams (often consisting of staff and volunteers but sometimes just volunteers) to create the products, services, or results known as projects. The project manager is the leader of the team and the person responsible for accomplishing the stated project objectives. In many cases "project manager" is a role and not a position or title. For example, if special events and direct mail campaigns are projects, the special events manager and the direct mail manager become project managers overseeing and guiding a series of projects during the year. These operations managers are still responsible for the day-to-day operations of their positions that aren't projects; they're just assuming the role of project manager to enable the project work to get done. Large nonprofits often have enough staff that projects are managed by professional project managers. Most nonprofits, however, rely on operations managers to manage projects.

The project manager has his or her eye on achieving specific objectives that are clearly identified: Raise three million dollars by the end of this fiscal year; increase membership in our association by 20 percent before the end of the quarter. The project manager asks the organization: "What is the specific desired outcome from this undertaking? What resources, budget, and time-frame do we have to achieve that outcome? What are the constraints within which we need to stay?" The project manager applies the tools and disciplines of project management to quickly develop a project plan identifying the activities needed to achieve the desired outcomes (see Chapter 6 for details on project planning). The project manager then puts that plan into action, monitoring and controlling the activities to ensure that expected outcomes are achieved. You'll find more about the desired attributes of a project manager in Chapter 8.

The Operations Manager

The operations manager, on the other hand, oversees the day-to-day operations of the organization. This entails oversight of the functions that keep the organization running: financial processing, donor acknowledgement, business correspondence, office management, long-term planning. Together the operations manager

Operations Manager	RESPONSIBILITIES	Project Manager
Responsible for department budget / overhead	Budget	Responsible for the project's budget (costs & revenue)
Responsible for the overall project portfolio & alignment of activities within it	Schedule	Responsible for project schedule
Responsible for volunteer database Responsible for volunteer position descriptions for the overall organization	Volunteers	Responsible for volunteer engagement Responsible for volunteer position descriptions as related to the project
Recruits, hires, assigns to projects; oversees performance on non-project activities	Staff Management	Oversees performance on project activities
Provides skill and career development	Skills Development	Provides training needed for project tasks

Figure 4.2. This table compares the responsibilities of an operations manager with those of a project manager.

and the various project managers make decisions relative to vacations, performance, and staff development, in the same manner they do now, but with additional tools and information. And, most importantly, they work together to determine how resources are allocated to the needs of the organization (see Figure 4.2).

Resource Allocation

In nonprofit project management, resources are the people (especially volunteers), equipment, and funding needed to complete the project. How well you manage your resources will determine whether you actually benefit from using project management. And the key to effective resource management is simple: agile nonprofits work on the projects that matter now. Just because a particular event was fruitful in the past doesn't mean that the event should be held again this year. Perhaps the cause supported by that event is no longer a strategic cause for your organization; perhaps that need has been adequately addressed and something else is more crucial, something that requires a different approach, a different project.

A prime example of agile resource management is the response to Hurricane Katrina by the American Red Cross. A significant priority at the time the hurricane occurred, the continued Katrina response, while certainly still important, became of lesser importance following the earthquake in Haiti in 2010. Priorities shifted, and the projects undertaken by the Red Cross needed to shift accordingly. Another example, on a smaller scale, involved a local road race sponsored by the local PTA to support the development of a new playground. Once the playground was established, the need for that race no longer existed. Instead the PTA faced a need to raise monies for the school library. The *chief development officer* and the

 GLOSSARY

Chief development officer is used in this book to identify the individual who is leading the nonprofit organization and who has fiscal responsibility for the organization. In some organizations this might be a director or a vice president of philanthropy.

board of directors might have decided that the road race would be a great way to satisfy that need, or they might have determined that a book sale would be more appropriate. Should they continue with the road race, perhaps using that to raise monies to maintain the playground? Which project they choose is not important here; what is important is that there needs to be a deliberate discussion about the projects, the resources required, and their relative priority.

Nonprofits often don't focus their efforts on what truly matters, projects that will have the most significant impacts on their strategic goals. Instead they focus on the projects that volunteers want to undertake or the community anticipates based on past years, such as the annual family day that supports a well-endowed childcare center (not part of the strategic plan for the year) versus a five-mile walk in support of the senior center (the priority for the organization). Many organizations will say "But we have a strategic plan we're following." Yet, their projects are not aligned with that plan. My personal experience has shown me that few organizations make the hard day-to-day decisions needed in choosing between priorities based on those strategic objectives.

 GLOSSARY

A *project portfolio* **is a collection of active and desired projects that consume an organization's resources.**

It's not that they don't do good work; it's that they don't really have a grasp of which projects are more important than other projects. Their resources are spread too thin and the most important projects suffer because of that lack of focus. The use of a *project portfolio* could help the operations manager and the project manager determine priority when deciding who works on what.

Chapter 14 provides advice on how to manage your project portfolio so that you focus your efforts on the most important projects.

Volunteer and Staff Responsibilities

A unique challenge facing nonprofits is their reliance on volunteers to assist staff. It's common for your development office to have more project work than people available to do the work. That's when volunteers and volunteer committees are brought into the picture. Although volunteers are occasionally asked to perform operational tasks, such as answering the telephone or assisting with correspondence, they're more often assigned project work. But volunteers aren't staff members. They're motivated differently, and they have different needs. Volunteers are not compensated financially. As one of my volunteer peers put it: "We're paid in hugs and smiles."

Her motivation to volunteer is the desire to make a difference in the life of another being. Another motivator frequently expressed, especially by older volunteers, is achieving a sense of usefulness, of still making a contribution. The smart manager will recognize this and bear these needs and motivations in mind when inviting a volunteer to undertake a piece of work.

Though the volunteer's skills and passions need to be considered when making assignments, it's also important to recognize which projects and project activities aren't suitable for a volunteer. For instance, asking the CEO of a major corporation to be a special events sponsor is perhaps something that's best done by a senior development staff member, or a board member, so that appropriate cultivation and stewardship can occur. It's certainly not a task appropriate for a first-time volunteer. And volunteers should always be viewed as temporary workers; remember, they're not committed to the organization the same way a paid employee is. Any project activity that has a life that extends over a period of time might not be appropriate for a volunteer.

Certainly anything pertaining to fiscal responsibilities (approving payments, acknowledging gifts, etc.) should be considered a task for staff only. This would ensure that the organization's fiduciary responsibilities are not compromised and that policies are strictly followed.

Volunteers should be reflected in your organization's overall resource pool, which lists all the resources — staff, volunteers, equipment, etc. — available for projects. The resource pool should include a list of volunteers, similar to an employee database, with information about the volunteer's skills and abilities, interests, and general availability to work on projects. A documented resource pool will enable the project manager in need of resources to invite qualified and interested volunteers to work on your organization's priorities. Using a resource pool, in conjunction with the organization's project portfolio, also curbs those "volunteer pet projects" that don't align with your organization's strategy. The resource pool will show you a list of a volunteer's desires and skills so that you can match that volunteer with the organization's desired projects, providing them with valuable work so they don't go off and create less valuable projects on their own.

Summary

Adopting project management practices in your organization doesn't eliminate the role of the operations manager. Rather, it augments the role with a dedicated leader, a project manager, whose focus is on achieving a specific, well-defined objective and overseeing the efforts of a team composed of staff and volunteers who will work on that project. The use of a project portfolio and associated project management practices will allow your organization to allocate its resources, and thereby the work, to those activities and projects that contribute most significantly to the achievement of your organization's strategic objectives. In other words, the operations manager and the project manager work together to ensure that the right person is assigned to the right job, at the right time.

5

Project Management Practices

In Chapter 4, we defined a project as "a temporary endeavor undertaken to create a unique product, service, or result" (Project Management Institute, 2013), and we identified several activities that are projects — special events, fundraising drives, volunteer recruitment campaigns. A capital fund campaign can be considered a series of related projects with a common goal (known as a program). As you can see, much of the work in running a nonprofit is project work, and whatever you can do to help you manage your projects better will enhance your nonprofit's overall performance. That's why project management is so important

The Project Management Institute (2013) defines project management as "the application of knowledge, skills, tools, and techniques to project activities in order to meet or exceed stakeholder needs and expectations from a project." Project management is a process that comprises five main phases that all projects go through: initiating, planning, executing, monitoring and controlling, and closing. In the initiating phase you define the new project and obtain authorization to start it. In the planning phase you establish the *scope* of the project, refine the objectives, and plan the actions required to achieve the project's objectives. In the executing phase you build your team of people, you acquire the other resources you need, and together you carry out the activities needed to complete the work defined in the plan. In the monitoring and controlling phase you regularly measure and monitor the progress of the project, identify any areas where changes to the plan might be needed, and make those changes. In the closing phase you formally accept the product, service or results, bring the project to a close, and gather any lessons you've learned in managing the project.

 GLOSSARY

Scope is the products, services, and results expected from a project.

In managing your project, you don't go through these phases sequentially; rather the phases are often iterative and often overlap (see Figure 5.1). But learning and applying the practices associated with these five project phases, especially planning, will help you better manage your projects.

Start It Right!

Project success can usually be attributed to managing the appropriate initiation and planning activities well. Often people are inclined to dive right into a project's core activities as soon as they're asked to do something. The gun has gone off; the race has started; and off they go. We forget, however, that the most successful runners have already run the race in their minds, they've planned their race. They know the challenges they'll face on that particular course and they've already developed approaches to overcome them. They know where the watering stations and check-in points are located. They know when they'll sprint and when they'll walk. The less successful runners will just race when they hear the starting gun, without a well-thought-out plan.

This tendency to immediately start racing is no different for nonprofit managers interested in the outcomes of their projects.

THE FIVE PROJECT MANAGEMENT PHASES

```
┌──────────────┐
│  Initiating  │◄─────────┐     ┌──────────────┐
└──────┬───────┘          │     │              │
       │                  │     │              │
       ▼                  │     │              │
┌──────────────┐          │     │  Monitoring  │
│   Planning   ├──────────┼────►│     and      │
└──┬────────▲──┘          │     │  Controlling │
   │        │             │     │              │
   ▼        │             │     │              │
┌──────────────┐          │     │              │
│  Executing   │◄─────────┤     │              │
└──────┬───────┘          │     │              │
       │                  │     │              │
       └──────────────────┼────►│              │
┌──────────────┐          │     │              │
│   Closing    │◄─────────┘     │              │
└──────────────┘                └──────────────┘
```

Figure 5.1. In managing projects, you generally proceed sequentially, from initiating to planning, executing, and finally closing the project, while monitoring and controlling along the way. But project management is highly iterative, as shown by the connecting lines. And if you're an agile nonprofit, you'll replan often as information and project requirements change.

But when managing a project like a special event or an appeal, it's important to clearly understand the scope of the activity before starting in order to ensure that the right goal is indeed reached. Like the successful runner, the successful nonprofit manager needs a well-thought-out plan for managing the project rather than simply doing it.

It's also equally important to identify a single person to serve as the project manager to organize and lead the committee, the team that will do the work needed to complete the project and to deliver its desired results. We often hear the phrase "one button to push," meaning one person in charge. This is the individual who can speak with authority about the project and who is empowered by the organization to make certain project-related decisions, such

29

as who does what activity. For the remainder of this book, we're going to assume that you are the project manager.

Set the Stage for Your Project

When contemplating a new project, the first action the project sponsor (board trustee, chief development officer, director, etc.) should undertake is the assignment of a staff member to serve as the project manager. The assigned individual, be it an event manager or direct mail manager or campaign manager, should meet with the project sponsor to obtain a clear understanding of the project's objectives including how success will be measured — dollars raised, donors in attendance, money spent to raise a dollar, volunteers signed up, facility built on time and under budget. See Figure 5.2 for information on developing your objectives.

 GLOSSARY

A *project charter* is a document signed by the project sponsor authorizing a project and giving the project manager the authority to use the organization's resources on the project's activities.

Once you've been assigned as the project manager and you clearly understand the objectives of the project, you need to begin developing what's known as a *project charter* and a *project scope statement.* I recommend that you create a project charter and scope statement as part of a more comprehensive document, a project guidance document (see Figure 5.3). In the project guidance document you first identify the purpose of the project, why it's being undertaken, and determine the project's stakeholders — that is, who will be affected by the project and what their interests in the project are. Gathering this information

 GLOSSARY

A *project scope statement* is a statement describing the work to be performed to deliver a product or service. It usually includes specified features and functions. An example of such a feature might be a "sit-down evening meal."

SMART PROJECT OBJECTIVES

- **SPECIFIC.** You want your objectives to be clear and unambiguous — what's to be done, why it's important, who's involved, and what the results look like. Be sure all your stakeholders can understand your objectives.

- **MEASURABLE.** You need definite criteria for measuring progress toward meeting your objectives, otherwise you will not know whether you've accomplished your goals. Criteria could be quantities, quality, frequency, costs, and/or deadlines.

- **ATTAINABLE.** Your objectives need to be realistic. If they're not, they're meaningless and will demotivate those trying to attain them. Ask whether there are sufficient resources available to accomplish your objectives and whether your team can actually do what's asked of them.

- **RESULTS-BASED.** Your objectives must deliver results that matter to you and your organization. Results-based objectives motivate your team to achieve them, and they motivate other stakeholders to support you.

- **TIME-SPECIFIC.** Your objectives need target dates. Committing to deadlines helps your team focus their efforts on meeting those objectives by those critical dates. Be sure to consider whether it's feasible to meet the deadlines.

Figure 5.2. SMART is a mnemonic to guide you when you set your project objectives. You want your objectives to be — Specific, Measurable, Attainable, Results-based, and Time-specific.

will help you determine who has the authority to make what decisions relative to your project and its outcomes.

Next you need to define the scope of your project. As the project manager, you and the project sponsor need to meet with the project stakeholders to discuss why the project is being undertaken (is its purpose to raise funds, to promote stewardship, to heighten community awareness?) and to determine what its boundaries are. By this I mean that if your project is a community awareness event, is the follow-up appeal to be considered part of the event? If your project is a golf tournament, is lunch with your nonprofit's executives that day part of the tournament or is that a separate event? You'll need to address who is empowered to make what decisions

31

PROJECT GUIDANCE DOCUMENT

Purpose: The Project Guidance Document indicates that a project has been preliminarily sanctioned by the organization and that resources can be used to further define and plan the details of that project. The document describes the vision, scope, authority, and project deliverables, as agreed upon by the Project Sponsor and other stakeholders.

PROJECT IDENTIFICATION

Project Name	Project Number	Date Created

Project Sponsor	Project Owner

Program Manager	Project Manager

PROJECT OVERVIEW

Project Background

< The background should provide an understanding of the events leading up to the project. It explains the history of the project, including any other times this kind of project has been undertaken. >

Business Needs

< Document the business needs behind the project. This could include the case statement used to obtain project approval. This should explain why the project is being done. >

Project Objectives

< Describe the objectives of the project and its deliverables. All projects should support and tie to strategic goals. The objectives should be SMART (Specific, Measurable, Attainable, Results-based, and Time-specific (see Figure 5.2)). >

Deliverable Description

< Describe what the project outcome will look like — a special event, an appeals mailing, or a new technology. Include any financial deliverables such as expected funds raised or additional donors acquired. >

Key Dates and Milestones

< List key dates and milestones that are required for the project. This could include any media dates or pre-event activities such as sponsor breakfasts. >

ORGANIZATIONAL CONSIDERATIONS

< Describe the departments and groups, including volunteers, that will be involved in the project. If the project manager has been identified, he or she should be included here. >

BUSINESS CASE

< Provide a summary budget, expected benefits, and cost of dollar raised anticipated for the project. Include a discussion of any alternative options that were discussed. >

Figure 5.3. Project governance document template with instructions.

SCOPE DEFINITION
< Specifically state those activities and deliverables that are within the boundaries of this project, and identify those that are not. For instance, development of mailing collateral might not be in scope for the project since the project will be using standard organizational pieces. However, development of specific marketing posters might be in scope. >

RISK IDENTIFICATION
< List in bullet format any known risks that might occur if the project proceeds and if it doesn't proceed. Include any thoughts relative to mitigation plans. These risks and plans will be elaborated upon in the next phase when the project team performs its risk analysis activities. >

ASSUMPTIONS AND CONSTRAINTS
< List in bullet format the known assumptions and constraints that have the potential to impact the project. List any assumptions and constraints that have been made in recommendations for the purpose of project planning. >

ACCEPTANCE CRITERIA
< Describe how the project will be periodically reviewed and which organization(s) have final approval authority. Describe what project success would look like. >

NECESSARY TO PROCEED
Next Phase Activities/Resources — required to move to the next phase, planning
< Describe the high-level activities and required resources (including volunteer) needed to do the next level of planning. The goal is to ensure availability of needed resources. These will also be tracked if the project does not continue. >

APPROVAL			
Name	Title	Date	Approved

ATTACHMENTS, AS APPLICABLE
< List any documents that support the information in this document. >

Figure 5.3 continued. Project governance document template with instructions.

relative to your project's deliverables, schedule, and budget. These decisions are then captured in the project guidance document, and all other project management documents will be based on this baseline information.

This use of a formal project guidance document ensures that you, the project sponsor, and project stakeholders have achieved a common understanding of the project's expected outcomes, what's in scope and what's out of scope, and who can make what decisions. It's a critically important document that encourages you to "do it right the first time" and assists in eliminating any confusion as the project progresses. Figure 5.4 shows you what the project overview might look like in your project guidance document for a sponsor dinner.

Plan It!

When you and the project sponsor and stakeholders are satisfied with the project guidance document and have signed off on it, you can begin planning the project's details. These plans include developing the project's *work breakdown structure* (discussed in Chapter 6), identifying the specific roles and responsibilities of staff, volunteers, and beneficiaries (especially as they relate to budget and schedule), acquiring and developing the project team, working with that team to develop the project's schedule, identifying milestones, identifying risks and plans for mitigating those risks, working up project budgets, and planning for the project's on-going communications. It's in doing these activities well that you really have a chance to ensure the project's success. We'll explore these activities in detail in subsequent chapters. Suffice it to say that knowing who will perform what activities at what time, how much financial support is available for your project, and understanding the risks associated with the plan, is critical to the eventual success of the project. It's equally critical to that success to understand and implement a communications plan that addresses the needs of those interested in the project. See Figure 5.5 for a description of the documents found in a comprehensive project plan.

 GLOSSARY

A *work breakdown structure* is a hierarchical decomposition of the work to be performed by the project team to create the expected project outcomes.

PROJECT GUIDANCE DOCUMENT

PROJECT IDENTIFICATION

Project Name	Project Number	Date Created
Sponsor Dinner (July 20)		20110301
Project Sponsor	Project Owner	
Dr. Susan Smith	Jane Woods	
Program Manager	Project Manager / Team Member / Role	
	James Dawe (Project Manager)	

PROJECT OVERVIEW

Project Background

This summer event is held annually to recognize those individuals who have supported the Society during the year and to encourage their continued support of the research we perform. It typically includes a catered sit-down meal in addition to a cocktail reception. Attendees will include the Society's board members and the organization's officers. Tables and individual tickets are sold to the community so that they can participate in the recognition. Selected guests are comp'd for attendance. In the past, ticket sales for this dinner have yielded $25K to $30K to the Society.

Business Needs

To recognize Society supporters, to share updates on our accomplishments and on our current research, to highlight opportunities for further support.

Project Objectives

- Sell 350 tickets by June 15 to accommodate caterer's schedule and to achieve financial goals
- Determine top ten sponsors and arrange for all ten to be present at dinner
- Select three research accomplishments and arrange for all three researchers to be present at dinner

Deliverable Description

A cocktail reception and catered sit-down meal, with an after dinner program of recognition and research presentations. Appropriate music can be played during the reception and dinner.

Key Dates and Milestones

- April 15 – Dinner location finalized
- May 1 – Final program of speakers and award recipients for marketing materials
- May 14 – Start ticket sales
- June 15 – Final ticket sales and headcount for caterer
- July 20 – Host the dinner
- July 31 – Final project accounting and close-out

Figure 5.4. Project overview section of a project guidance document for a sponsor dinner.

35

PROJECT MANAGEMENT PLAN

1 INTRODUCTION

< Provide a sentence or two introducing the project, its sponsor, and its purpose. >

2 PROJECT INFORMATION

< Provide a brief paragraph describing the project. It should provide a summary of the events leading up to the project and its expected outcomes. >

3 PROJECT MANAGEMENT APPROACH

< Identify the project sponsor, project owner, project manager, and deputy project manager if applicable. Provide contact information for each member of the project management team. >

4 PROJECT SCOPE

< Discuss the project scope. Describe the purpose of the project, its objectives, and its outcomes. >

5 PROJECT DELIVERABLES

< List the project's deliverables. Internal deliverables are those internal to the project, such as marketing materials used to sell event tickets; external deliverables are items provided to others, such as printed programs for a concert or the final tickets sent to participants. >
- 5.1 Internal Deliverables
- 5.2 External Deliverables

6 PROJECT ORGANIZATION STRUCTURE

< Depict the project team's organizational structure with either a project team roster or organizational chart. Identify each team member and associated role. >

7 COMMUNICATIONS PLAN AND MATRIX

< Address project team communications protocols and methods. If using technology, identify URLs and processes to obtain access. Include a communications matrix depicting when certain standard meetings will occur and who participates, and when status reports will be provided and their distribution. Include project team contact information. >
- 7.1 Project Team and Stakeholder Contact Information

8 SCOPE MANAGEMENT PLAN

< Describe how project scope will be managed — who is authorized to approve changes and how change requests will be reviewed and accepted. >
- 8.1 Scope Statement
- 8.2 Scope Management Roles and Responsibilities
- 8.3 Scope Control
- 8.4 Scope Verification

Figure 5.5. This figure lists the documents that comprise the project plan with instructions. If your project is small, with little risk to the organization, many of these documents are overkill. But you should at least consider how important any of these items might be in developing your project management plan.

9 BUDGET (COST) MANAGEMENT PLAN

< Describe how the project's budget will be managed — who is authorized to approve costs, how budget changes will be reviewed and accepted, and how frequently budget data will be updated. >
- 9.1 Budget Management Roles and Responsibilities
- 9.2 Budget Planning and Estimating
- 9.3 Budget Tracking
- 9.4 Budget Controls

10 SCHEDULE MANAGEMENT PLAN

< Describe how the project's schedule will be managed — who is authorized to approve schedule changes such as vacation requests received from staff assigned to the project, how schedule changes will be communicated, and how frequently the schedule will be updated. >
- 10.1 Schedule Management Roles and Responsibilities
- 10.2 Schedule Management Approach

11 RESOURCE MANAGEMENT PLAN

< Describe how the project's resources will be managed — who is authorized to approve changes in assignments and how new team members will be oriented to the project. >
- 11.1 Resource Management Roles and Responsibilities
- 11.2 Resource Orientation
- 11.3 Resource Training

12 RISK MANAGEMENT PLAN

< Discuss how the project's risks will be managed — how often they will be reviewed by the project team and the sponsor, who is authorized to invoke a mitigation plan, and how the risk's occurrence will be communicated and documented for other projects. >
- 12.1 Risk Management Roles and Responsibilities
- 12.2 Risk Management Process
- 12.3 Risk Documentation

13 QUALITY MANAGEMENT PLAN

< Describe how the quality of the project's activities and outputs will be managed — who will review and approve deliverables.>
- 13.1 Quality Management Roles and Responsibilities
- 13.2 Quality Management Process

14 VENDOR MANAGEMENT PLAN

< Discuss how any vendors used to support the project will be managed — who has the authority to negotiate contracts and prices and who oversees the vendor's activities, including approving invoices and accepting products or services provided. >
- 14.1 Vendor Management Roles and Responsibilities
- 14.2 Vendor Acquisition Process
- 14.3 Vendor Invoicing Process

Figure 5.5 continued. The documents that comprise the project plan.

The Project Life Cycle Model — The Project's Framework for Success

An important step in planning your project is to identify what methodology or processes you need to follow to facilitate project success. That is, you need to develop a framework to guide you — what's called a project life cycle model. A project life cycle is "a collection of project phases, serving to define the beginning and end of a project" (Project Management Institute, 2013). The model simply shows you how to proceed through those phases to complete your project.

One question that should be asked but often isn't when determining whether you should follow a particular set of processes to accomplish something is "Why? What's broken that following the new processes would fix?" We're often told the reason is to make sure that everyone in the organization does work in the same way, consistently, using the same language. When we probe further about why this consistency is needed (after all, no one is in business for consistency), we're told that, if everyone works the same way, should someone leave a position, someone else could step in and assume the role. Ahh! Now we're talking about something different — we're talking about risk mitigation. That is, the reason to acquire or develop and apply repeatable management processes is to ensure consistency of practice, so that everyone follows the same process, so that vacancies can be filled with little disruption to a project. Overemphasizing this consistency of practice has made many managers shy away from using project management. They fear that project management will be too burdensome, that so much effort will be wasted on trying to follow the "right" process that important work won't get done.

But projects aren't identical and they don't have the same risks. So why do we require them to use all the exact same processes, to follow the same degree of rigor? Project success is more likely to happen, the risks more likely to be averted, if a project is established with its own project life cycle model, one that embraces both traditional and agile project management processes that are appropriate to the type of project and the risks involved. You (the project manager), the project sponsor, and the project planning team (the people doing the planning, which might be a subset of the overall team that will work on the project) should together determine which processes are needed to support project success. That is, together you should establish the project's overall framework, the project's life cycle model.

 **GLOSSARY**

A *methodology* is a collection of practices, techniques, and procedures used by individuals performing a discipline.

A project life cycle model is specific to a project, while a methodology is typically specific to an organization. A well-written *methodology* is able to support multiple project life cycle models. One of the tools a project management team has at its disposal is the ability to develop a project life cycle model by drawing from multiple methodologies based on the requirements of the project, to ensure critical processes are not overlooked by the project team. The savvy project manager adapts methodologies as needed to fit the risks and requirements of the project at hand.

Let's explore that last sentence a bit further: The savvy project manager adapts methodologies as needed to fit the risks and requirements of the project at hand. This means that you and your project planning team should understand the requirements of the project and the associated risks. You can then research your organization for methodologies, guidelines, handbooks, or subject matter experts for advice as to what activities are needed to fulfill the project requirements.

Establish Your Project Life Cycle Model

When planning a project life cycle model, your project planning team should apply a top-down approach, first considering the highest-level, major activities required by the project. This usually

39

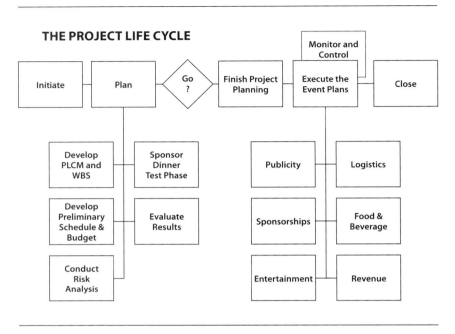

THE PROJECT LIFE CYCLE

Figure 5.6. Project life cycle model for a sponsor dinner.

starts by addressing the activities needed during the five discrete phases of the project: initiating, planning, executing, monitoring and controlling, and closing.

One question that your project team needs to consider at this point is: How do you break your project up into smaller chunks so that you can better manage it, staff it, or demonstrate to your sponsor that the project is going along just fine? Keep this question in mind as you develop your project life cycle model.

While a project typically has only one initiation phase, it might be desirable for a specific project to have the project team use a life cycle that has two initiation phases. For example, holding a new special event might be a project that follows this particular life cycle model. In this example, the project sponsor identifies that obtaining sufficient community sponsorship for the event is a risk. Your project planning team, including the sponsor, has discussed

40

this and determined that hosting a preliminary event to test the community would be an acceptable means to determine if the risk truly exists. Your project's initial planning and execution activities are related to the planning and hosting of a sponsorship solicitation dinner; if the response from that dinner is positive, then your project sponsor can make an informed decision and advise the project team to proceed with the planning and execution of the project resulting in the actual special event. Your project closes after that event.

In this case, your special events project life cycle model might look like Figure 5.6. By doing some preliminary planning and testing sponsorship, your project team is able to avert the potential risk associated with the special event not having the required community support.

Then What?

After the project life cycle model is mapped out, your project planning team should review the actual work needed to be performed during the project's execution phase. This is where the detailed planning described in Chapter 6 starts to come into play. Your project planning team determines the types of work likely to be needed to complete the project and whether similar work has been performed in the past.

I've presented a simple example of a project life cycle model. While it might look like a cumbersome activity, developing a project life cycle model can usually be accomplished rather quickly, and the return on the investment of time is high. In most businesses, proper risk mitigation can be the difference between a project's economic success and failure. By planning your project's overall life, by thinking in a non-sequential mode and leveraging the appropriate processes from diverse methodologies, handbooks, and other sources, your project team can develop a project life cycle model that's as unique as the project they're undertaking and one that encourages overall project success. This project life cycle model can then be used as the basis for the more detailed planning discussed in Chapter 6.

Monitor, Control, and Communicate, Communicate, Communicate!

As the project proceeds, you, the project manager, monitor and control it, making timely decisions to ensure that your project's objectives are achieved. You'll also keep all stakeholders informed as to the project's progress, ensuring that there are no surprises. You need to periodically review the project scope statement with the volunteers and staff working on the project, to remind them of the project's scope and objectives. Should the project's stakeholders change the project's objectives (for example, increase the financial goals of the event), your project team must be told because the project plan needs to be reviewed to determine if other changes are needed to achieve the new objectives. The project team should understand what the changes mean in terms of resources, time commitments, and budgets. If increases in any of these items are needed, you must address these needs with the project stakeholders and obtain the project sponsor's approval of any changes before proceeding. And any changes to the project's original plan should be documented for use in the future.

Throughout the life of the project (the planning of the event, the actual event itself, and the closing of the event), you'll also implement the project's communications plan (discussed in Chapter 7). This typically includes receiving status reports from volunteers and staff on a regular basis, consolidating them, and generating appropriate status reports to stakeholders. These reports could be internal memos, letters to the community, or articles in an employee newsletter. At a minimum, the status report should report about the various criteria identified as important to the project (see Figure 5.7).

PROJECT STATUS REPORT

PROJECT IDENTIFICATION

Project Name	Project Number	For the Period Covering
Sponsor Dinner (July 20)		20110401 - 20110415
Project Sponsor	Project Owner	
Dr. Susan Smith	Jane Woods	
Program Manager	Project Manager / Team Member / Role	
	James Dawe (Project Manager)	

ACCOMPLISHMENTS   (12 HOURS TO DATE)

TASK: Meetings
Hours this Week: 2 hrs   Hours to Date: 4 hrs   Estimated Hours Remaining: 8 hrs
- Prepared for and participated in monthly team meeting
- Met with Dr. Smith and Ellen (responsible for catering) to determine dinner locations

TASK: Project Management
Hours this week: 2 hrs   Hours to Date: 8 hrs   Estimated Hours Remaining: 40 hrs
- Updated project schedule and budget (1 hr)
- Interviewed volunteer candidate for invitation design work (1 hr)

TASK: Sponsorship Identification
Hours this week: 0 hrs   Hours to Date: 0 hrs   Estimated Hours Remaining: 20 hrs
- No activity this week

ACTIVITIES PLANNED FOR NEXT TWO WEEKS

TASK: Meetings
- Status meeting with Jane Woods

TASK: Project Management
- Fill remaining team positions (Design Work, Sponsorship)
- Maintain budget and schedule; update risk log
- Respond to team members as needed

TASK: Sponsorship Identification
- Identify preliminary list of potential sponsors & review same with Dr. Smith

ISSUES REQUIRING RESOLUTION

Description	Priority	Resolution Date	Owner	Status
Dr. Smith traveling and unavailable entire month of June	#1	5/1/11	Dr. Smith	Dr. Smith identifying a staff member to cover.

LOST TIME (HOURS, CAUSE AND PLAN TO RECOVER)

None

Figure 5.7. Project status report for a sponsor dinner.

43

Don't Run to the Next Project!

There is a tendency to celebrate the successful completion of an event or an appeal and then move on to the next one, overlooking the critical step of closing out the project. A proper closeout would include not only closing the financial aspects of the event but also conducting a final team meeting. The purpose of this meeting is to capture valuable information about the project and to initiate the volunteer stewardship desired to support future projects. This meeting should include the extended project team, including the project's requestor. You should capture all lessons learned, including those elements that worked well and should be repeated and those that didn't work well and shouldn't be repeated.

Summary

Project management is a unique discipline focused on the successful achievement of a stated goal or objective. The application of project management does not need to be an exercise in the application of more overhead. Rather, it needs to be the practical application of those project management knowledge areas and skills required to ensure that a project — special event, an appeal, or a volunteer search — achieves the desired goals. Careful attention upfront to defining and planning the project, exercising timely attention to the progress of the project, communicating information about the project, and capturing lessons learned for the future can assist in preventing costly oversights and mistakes.

6

Planning, Executing, Planning Some More

There's a common phrase about the best laid plans of mice and men — they oft go astray. However, that doesn't mean that planning doesn't have value. And in project management good planning can be the difference between success and failure. Proper project planning means determining the resources that you need and the work that needs to be executed in order to accomplish a specific objective. It also requires that you understand the things that might cause your plans to be insufficient before you actually start "the doing."

Planning enables your team to develop a roadmap of the project, to know what's expected to happen when, how the pieces fit together, and where there is risk. Planning assists you in eliminating some of the surprises that can derail your project. A properly thought-out plan can result in a well-executed project that achieves its stated goals without staff and volunteer burn-out.

Where Do You Begin?

As we mentioned in Chapter 5, your initial project planning begins with the development of the project life cycle model, the high-level framework that guides you as to how the project's activities will be accomplished and its objectives achieved. In the next step in planning the project you need to identify the necessary activities and the amount of work each activity requires, determine when each activity needs to occur, and, finally, identify who will perform the activity.

This more detailed planning begins with your project planning team developing a project work breakdown structure. A project WBS is a list of the pieces of work, small enough to be manageable, that you need to have accomplished in order to achieve your project's objectives. These pieces of work are included in the project schedule. Figure 6.1 shows you a WBS for your special event, a sponsor dinner.

The list is hierarchical and starts at the top with the end objective of the project (say the sponsor dinner) and is then subdivided into manageable components. Note that the first level in the hierarchy (the objective is considered the zero level) consists of the discrete project phases identified in your special events project life cycle model. Each phase is further broken down into the activities needed to complete the work. Your project planning team determines the first and second levels of this WBS, identifying the types of work likely to be needed in each. In developing the lower levels of the WBS the team should consult staff members or volunteers in your organization who are knowledgeable about the detailed work involved in each activity to ensure that all the work needed has been considered.

The WBS also provides a structure for budget tracking. A general rule of thumb for when you develop a WBS is to break down the work into activities that can be accomplished within forty to eighty hours, or the level at which project costs are tracked. Breaking down the work into this level of effort permits the assigned staff member or volunteer the ability to feel a sense

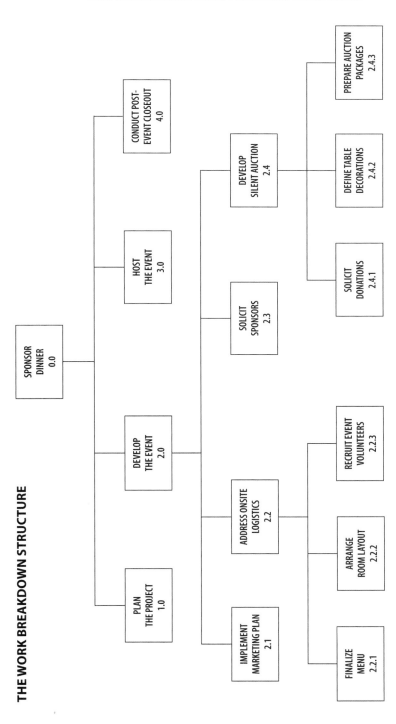

Figure 6.1. Work breakdown structure for a sponsor dinner. A WBS identifies the manageable pieces of work that need to be accomplished in order to achieve the project's objectives.

of immediacy associated with a due date as well as a sense of accomplishment at least every other week.

Continuing with our event example, let's assume the initial objective is indeed a sponsorship dinner. If your organization is a nonprofit, chances are they have hosted dinners in the past for executives or other dignitaries. The project planning team can obtain the processes and *project artifacts* that were applied for a previous successful dinner. These processes are then inserted into the current project's WBS as activities to be performed when the project team actually prepares for that dinner event. Another major piece of work in the special event project would be publicity — the creation of posters, press releases and other collateral. Again, your organization most likely has a defined set of processes that the Public Affairs Department always applies when doing work for the organization. Your special event project team will leverage that knowledge, rather than try to identify the necessary activities on their own.

 GLOSSARY

Project artifacts are the documents and other items produced by the project team throughout the life of the project.

By continuing in this mode, your project planning team can quickly identify and include in your WBS those activities that have been required for success in the past. They can have a degree of assurance that they have not overlooked any crucial work and that they have a WBS that's tailored to address the unique requirements of your particular project.

While planning work at this level of detail might look like a cumbersome activity to complete, the return on investment in developing a work breakdown structure and using it as the basis for building your project's schedule and budget is invaluable. This level of planning is also priceless when it's time to assign staff and volunteers to specific activities. Using the WBS ensures that no critical activity is overlooked.

☑ QUICK TIP — THE PROJECT WALL

One method I've found useful in creating a WBS is to establish a project wall. I start by first establishing the top level of the work breakdown structure on the wall, using one color of sticky notes. I write the name of the project phase on the note and place it on the wall. I then assign each person, or work group, involved in my project a different color note. Team members are asked to write a single verb/noun combination on the sticky note, describing a project activity to be performed by that person, an activity that can be accomplished in less than two weeks. For instance, "design invitations" might be something the person overseeing communications might have. That individual might also have the activity "draft invitation letter." The individual responsible for the mailing might have "generate labels" as an activity in her color. As activity notes are created, they are placed on the wall, where the project manager attempts to group them into the work breakdown structure. Figure 6.2 shows a sample of a project wall in work. We keep creating activity notes until we think we have identified all the work.

Estimate the Effort

Now that the planning team, including you and the project sponsor, has a clear picture of the work involved in the project, they can begin to estimate how much work is needed to complete each activity.

Estimating the work required to complete an activity is perhaps the hardest task in planning a project. Often it's because we're estimating the effort of someone else, we're estimating an activity we've never performed in the past, or we're thinking in terms of duration, not effort. Effort is the amount of staff or volunteer time required to complete the activity. Effort is usually measured in

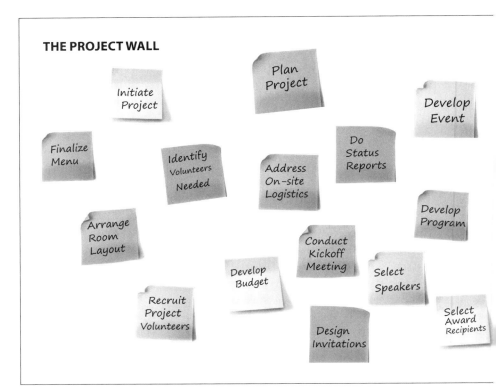

THE PROJECT WALL

Figure 6.2. Create a project wall. I've found this exercise extremely useful in developing the work breakdown structure. Create notes listing every activity you

hours and reflects uninterrupted time. So, when estimating effort it's important to factor out normal interruptions such as telephone calls and emails.

Duration is defined as the length of time it takes to complete an activity. When estimating duration, planners need to take into consideration the other work that the staff member or volunteer may be performing, including attending meetings, supporting other projects, doing operational work. Both estimates are used in planning, but first let's focus on effort.

The best method available to estimate the length of time it will take to accomplish an activity is to identify the effort involved in

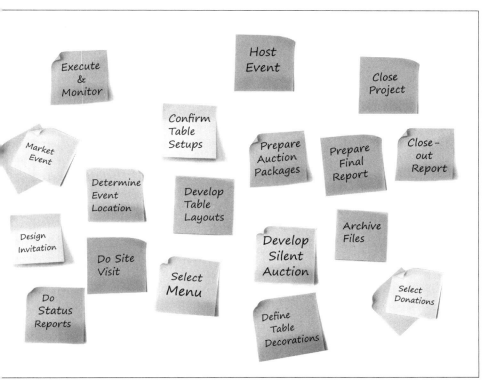

can think of that will be needed for the project and place them on the wall. Then you can group them into the categories that will make up the WBS.

completing a similar activity in the past. If you use this method, however, your team should always consider adjusting that effort estimate to reflect the skills of the person most likely to perform the activity this time. If past actual efforts are not available, or if this is the first time an activity is being undertaken, your team should probe its network to locate someone who has performed a similar activity in another environment. Frequently this means asking someone at another nonprofit what their experience was. When using this method, again, your team should adjust the esti-mate to reflect their inexperience in order to minimize some of the risk with the estimate.

51

 GLOSSARY

Work packages are the lowest level within the work breakdown structure for which duration and costs are estimated and managed. They can also represent work that is handed off to another entity to perform under a subcontract or other agreement.

Project management practitioners like to use an estimating method called weighted average in an attempt to minimize risk in the estimates. The weighted average method is based on obtaining the optimistic (shortest time/effort or least cost), pessimistic (longest time/effort or highest cost) and most likely (highest probability) estimates for *work packages*. It then takes a weighted average of the three to arrive at the estimated value. This method uses the following formula:

$$\text{Estimate} = \frac{\text{Pessimistic} + (4 \times \text{Most Likely}) + \text{Optimistic}}{6}$$

Your project team might consider applying this method to those activities with effort estimates that truly are guesses. In this scenario, each team member provides a number for the most optimistic, most pessimistic, and most likely estimates. You then take the average of each of these categories and apply that average to the formula.

Develop the Schedule

Now that your team, including you and the project sponsor, has a clear picture of the work and effort involved in the project, they can begin to determine how each activity fits into an overall project schedule and determine when the project can be completed. Note that this is when the project *can* be completed, not when it *will* be completed. Upon completion of this first pass at the schedule your team will refine their plan, if necessary, to achieve the project by the time it's needed.

After estimating the effort required to complete each activity, the first step in developing the project schedule is to put the work into its logical sequence, identifying which work needs to be completed before something else can start and which work can be performed in parallel. At this point you or the project sponsor should not constrain your planning team by saying "That's too much work for one person." Remember, people have not yet been assigned to the work.

After all the work has been put into sequence, the next step is to identify any "must-meet dates" as-

 QUICK TIP

As effort estimates are created for each activity, they should be written on the bottom of each sticky note on your project wall. This will support identifying how much effort is needed from each person involved in the project. It will also enable the project manager to verify that all work has been estimated.

sociated with any of the activities. These are those dates, or milestones as they are frequently called, that are driven by factors outside your project team's control. Common activities that might have such dates are the release of a proof to a printer within a given window during which they can print materials free of charge, or an annual board meeting during which gala tickets are distributed.

At this point you can determine the number of people you'll need to complete the project and resource assignments can be made. Your planning team can engage those people to estimate realistic durations, that is, start and end dates for each activity, factoring in those daily work interruptions, planned

 QUICK TIP

Take the sticky notes you used to develop the WBS and move them around on the wall to depict the sequence and parallelism.

vacations, staff retreats, and other activities that will take them away from the project. A general rule of thumb used by many in estimating is that a typical eight-hour workday will yield six hours of productive work effort. Some of those hours will be needed for normal operational work; what's left is what's available for project work. If an activity can be performed by a volunteer, that should also be noted in the WBS.

At this point, the project wall can be transferred into a project schedule tool, such as Microsoft Project, or into a spreadsheet for tracking. Milestones should be highlighted in that tool, so that the project team can focus on them. It is often useful to communicate schedule progress to project sponsors by showing progress towards the milestones, as opposed to showing schedule details. A milestone schedule is shown in Figure 6.3. Figure 6.4 shows a project schedule using a spreadsheet, with the milestones identified in italic. This is the schedule view that would be used in a project team meeting.

☑ QUICK TIP

I once more use the notes on my project wall to indicate volunteer activities by drawing or placing a red star on each sticky note that contains a volunteer activity. When a volunteer is identified and assigned to that activity, I write the volunteer's name on the note.

Plan the Project's Communications

One aspect of a project that's often overlooked is the time required to effectively communicate the project status to everyone interested. Attending staff meetings, making project presentations, writing an article for the organization's newsletter — these are all project activities that take time to accomplish and that should be reflected in the project's WBS.

Planning how team and stakeholder communications will be addressed on the project is one of the key responsibilities typically assigned to the project manager. Working with the project sponsor, you should determine the frequency and format by which you'll share project status updates. Together you and the project sponsor determine the frequency of formal stakeholder presentations and designate responsibility for preparation and delivery of those updates. You'll collaborate with the entire project team to determine the scheduling of team meetings, respecting the availability of volunteers to fully participate in the meetings. That probably

MILESTONE SCHEDULE FOR A SPONSOR DINNER

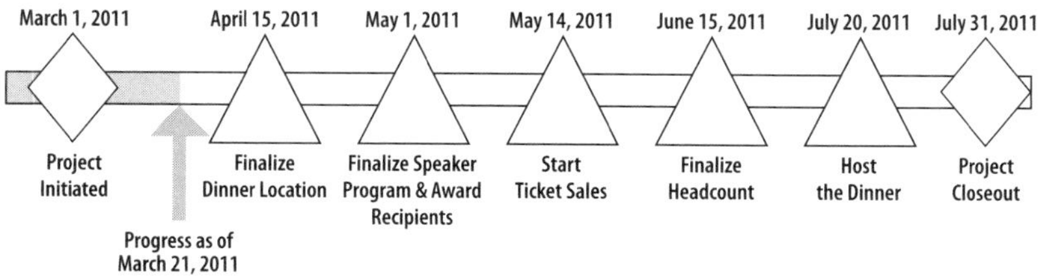

Figure 6.3. Milestones are critical events during the life of the project. You pay special attention to them so that if problems arise in meeting those deadlines you can take corrective action to get the overall project back on schedule.

means weekend or evening meetings at a location accessible by all volunteers. You should also address how communications will occur with team members not able to participate in meetings and between meetings. When working with volunteers, it's important to remember that not everyone has ready access to technology; do not assume e-mail will work for everyone in a timely manner or that everyone has a smartphone that can receive text messages. While working on a benefit for our local hospital, I had a young woman on the project team who didn't have access to a computer at home. She relied on the resources of the community library to check e-mails, something she was able to do only on Saturdays. If I needed to reach her to inform her of a meeting time change or get an update to her during the week, I knew I needed to call her. Another commonly overlooked assumption is that everyone carries a cell phone and is immediately available. Be sure to know how you can reach team members on short notice if you need to reschedule a meeting.

Figure 6.5 (on page 62) is an example of a communications matrix for your sponsor dinner project. It's a tool for keeping track of your project communications needs. Figure 6.6 describes in detail what information goes into a communications matrix.

PROJECT SCHEDULE—SPONSOR DINNER (JULY 20)									
WBS	Task Name	Effort Estimate	Duration	Start	Finish	Depen-dencies	Percent Complete	Assigned to	Actual Effort
1.0	Initiate the Project								
1.1	Develop Project Guidance document	4 hrs	1 day	3/1/2011	3/1/2011			PM	
1.2	Obtain resources								
1.2.1	• Establish project team structure	1 hr	1 day	3/1/2011	3/1/2011	1.1		PM	
1.2.2	• Recruit project team volunteers	6 hrs	10 days	3/1/2011	3/12/2011	1.2.1		PM	
1.3	Develop Project Mgmt Notebook								
1.3.1	• Develop Preliminary Risk Mgmt Plan	2 hrs	1 day	3/2/2011	3/2/2011	1.1		PM	
1.3.2	• Conduct Risk Analysis Session w/ volunteers & Dr Smith	2 hrs	1 day	3/13/2011	3/13/2011	1.3.1; 1.2		PM; Team	
1.3.3	• Update Risk Mgmt Plan	2 hrs	1 day	3/14/2011	3/14/2011	1.3.2		PM	
1.3.4	• Finalize Communications Plan	2 hrs	1 day	3/14/2011	3/14/2011	1.2		PM; Team	
1.4	Conduct project team kick-off	2 hrs	1 day	3/15/2011	3/15/2011	1.2; 1.3		PM	
1.5	Establish Milestone Schedule	.5 hr	1 day	3/16/2011	3/16/2011	1.4		PM	
1.6	Complete project schedule and budget	.5 hr	1 day	3/17/2011	3/17/2011	1.5		PM	

Figure 6.4. Detailed project schedule for a sponsor dinner.

PROJECT SCHEDULE—SPONSOR DINNER (continued)

WBS	Task Name	Effort Estimate	Duration	Start	Finish	Dependencies	Percent Complete	Assigned to	Actual Effort
2.0	**Plan the Event**								
2.1	**Determine the Location**								
2.1.1	• Research possible locations	2 hrs	1 day	3/18/2011	3/18/2011			Logistics Vol.	
2.1.2	• Conduct site visits	4 hrs	7 days	3/20/2011	3/27/2011			Logistics Vol.	
2.1.3	• Select dinner location	.5 hr	2 days	3/20/2011	3/31/2011			Logistics Vol.	
2.1.4	• Negotiate contract with facility	4 hrs	10 days	4/1/2011	4/15/2011			PM; Purchasing	
2.1.5	• *DINNER LOCATION DETERMINED*			*4/15/2011*	*4/15/2011*				
2.2	**Plan the Dinner**								
2.2.1	• Determine decoration needs (flowers, balloons, etc)	5 hrs	1 day	4/15/2011	4/15/2011			Logistics Vol.	
2.2.2	• Order decorations	.5 hr	1 day	4/15/2011	4/15/2011			Logistics Vol.	
2.2.3	• Arrange for caterer (same as last year)	2 hrs	1 day	4/16/2011	4/16/2011			Logistics Vol.	
2.2.4	• Review and select dinner menu	3 hrs	1 day	4/17/2011	4/17/2011			Logistics Vol.	

Figure 6.4 continued. Detailed project schedule for a sponsor dinner.

WBS	Task Name	Effort Estimate	Duration	Start	Finish	Dependencies	Percent Complete	Assigned to	Actual Effort
	PROJECT SCHEDULE — SPONSOR DINNER (continued)								
2.2.5	• *DINNER MENU FINALIZED*			*4/18/2011*	*4/18/2011*				
2.3	**Determine Honorees and Speakers**								
2.3.1	• Review on-going research programs	1 hr	1 day	4/15/2011	4/15/2011			Speaker Vol.	
2.3.2	• Review possible programs with Dr. Smith	1 hr	1 day	4/15/2011	4/15/2011			Speaker Vol.	
2.3.3	• Approve research selections	1 hr	1 day	4/16/2011	4/16/2011			Sponsor	
2.3.4	• Confirm speaker availability	1 hr	1 day	4/17/2011	4/17/2011			Speaker Vol.	
2.3.5	• Obtain names of top 10 sponsors from the donor database administrator	.5 hr	2 days	4/18/2011	4/19/2011			Speaker Vol.	
2.3.6	• Obtain VP approval of honorees	.5 hr	2 days	4/20/2011	4/21/2011			Speaker Vol.	
2.3.7	• *FINAL SPEAKER /HONOREE PROGRAM AVAILABLE*			*5/1/2011*	*5/1/2011*			Speaker Vol.	
2.4	**Prepare & Mail Invitations**								
2.4.1	• Craft honoree invitation letter	5 hrs	1 day	4/18/2011	4/18/2011			Ticket Vol.	
2.4.2	• Obtain VP approval of letter wording	1 hr	1 day	4/19/2011	4/19/2011			Sponsor	

Figure 6.4 continued. Detailed project schedule for a sponsor dinner.

58

PROJECT SCHEDULE—SPONSOR DINNER (continued)

WBS	Task Name	Effort Estimate	Duration	Start	Finish	Dependencies	Percent Complete	Assigned to	Actual Effort
2.4.3	• Print honoree invitation letter	5 hrs	3 days	4/19/2011	4/23/2011			Ticket Vol.	
2.4.4	• Mail honoree invitation letter	1 hr	1 day	4/24/2011	4/24/2011			Ticket Vol.	
2.4.5	• Design ticket invitation and wording	5 hrs	2 days	4/18/2011	4/19/2011			Ticket Vol.	
2.4.6	• Coordinate design with printer	1 hr	5 days	4/19/2011	4/24/2011			Ticket Vol.	
2.4.7	• VP review and approve invitations	1 hr	1 day	4/25/2011	4/25/2011			Ticket Vol.	
2.4.8	• Obtain mailing list from DBA	1 hr	2 days	4/19/2011	4/21/2011			DBA	
2.4.9	• VP review and approve mailing list	4 hrs	5 days	4/20/2011	4/24/2011			Sponsor	
2.4.10	• Print ticket invitations and envelopes	5 hrs	3 days	4/25/2011	4/30/2011			Ticket Vol.	
2.4.11	• Mail ticket invitations	1 hr	1 day	4/30/2011	4/30/2011			Ticket Vol.	
2.5	**Process Ticket Sales**								
2.5.1	• Receive RSVPs and track replies	30 hrs	30 days	5/14/2011	6/14/2011			Ticket Vol.	
2.5.2	• Create name tags for "Yes" replies	30 hrs	30 days	5/14/2011	6/14/2011			Ticket Vol.	
2.5.3	• Provide final count to caterer & facility	30 hrs	30 days	6/15/2011	6/15/2011			Logistics Vol	
2.5.4	• *CONCLUDE TICKET SALES*			*6/15/2011*	*6/15/2011*			Ticket Vol.	

Figure 6.4 continued. Detailed project schedule schedule for a sponsor dinner.

PROJECT SCHEDULE — SPONSOR DINNER (continued)

WBS	Task Name	Effort Estimate	Duration	Start	Finish	Dependencies	Percent Complete	Assigned to	Actual Effort
3.0	Conduct the Event								
3.1	Review table set-up & make corrections as needed	2 hrs	1 day	7/20/2011	7/20/2011			Logistics Vol.	
3.2	Support Dinner Registration Table (give name tags)	2 hrs	1 day	7/20/2011	7/20/2011			Ticket Vol.	
3.3	Staff Coat Check Room	4 hrs	1 day	7/20/2011	7/20/2011			"Day of" Volunteer	
3.4	Monitor caterer performance	4 hrs	1 day	7/20/2011	7/20/2011			Logistics Vol.	
3.5	Meet & greet speakers & honorees	2 hrs	1 day	7/20/2011	7/20/2011			Speaker Vol.; Sponsor	
3.5	Meet & greet attendees	2 hrs	1 day	7/20/2011	7/20/2011			PM; Project Owner	
4.0	Project Close-out								
4.1	Do Dinner Follow-up								
4.1.1	• Craft thank you notes to speakers	4 hrs	1 day	7/25/2011	7/25/2011			Speaker Vol.	

Figure 6.4 continued. Detailed project schedule for a sponsor dinner.

60

WBS	Task Name	Effort Estimate	Duration	Start	Finish	Depen-dencies	Percent Complete	Assigned to	Actual Effort
	PROJECT SCHEDULE—SPONSOR DINNER (continued)								
4.1.2	• Obtain Dr. Smith's approval of notes	1 hr	1 day	7/26/2011	7/26/2011			Speaker Vol.	
4.1.3	• Mail thank you notes	1 hr	1 day	7/26/2011	7/26/2011			Speaker Vol.	
4.1.4	• Craft thank you notes to volunteers	2 hrs	1 day	7/25/2011	7/25/2011			PM	
4.1.5	• Obtain Dr. Smith's approval of volunteer notes	1 hr	1 day	7/26/2011	7/26/2011			PM	
4.1.6	• Obtain Jane Wood's approval of volunteer notes	1 hr	1 day	7/26/2011	7/26/2011			PM	
4.1.7	• Mail thank you notes to volunteers	1 hr	1 day	7/26/2011	7/26/2011			PM	
4.2	**Prepare Financial Reports**								
4.2.1	• Obtain and process all final invoices	4 hrs	1 day	7/25/2011	7/25/2011			PM	
4.2.2	• Obtain ticket sales amounts from Accounting	1 hr	1 day	7/25/2011	7/25/2011			PM	
4.2.3	• Prepare final status report	3 hrs	1 day	7/27/2011	7/27/2011			PM	
4.3	**Finalize content of Project Mgmt Notebook**	2 hrs	1 day	7/28/2011	7/28/2011			PM	
4.4	Archive all correspondence related to project	2 hrs	1 day	7/31/2011	7/31/2011			PM	

Figure 6.4 continued. Detailed project schedule for a sponsor dinner.

61

COMMUNICATIONS MATRIX

PROJECT IDENTIFICATION

Project Name	Project Number	For the Period Covering
Sponsor Dinner		20110314 - 20110318
Project Sponsor	**Project Owner**	
Dr. Susan Smith	Jane Woods	
Program Manager	**Project Manager**	
	James Dawe	

Purpose: To identify project communication requirements that provide information on the sending and receiving of project data in a timely manner.

What	Source	By Whom	To Whom	By When	How	Why	Restrictions / Comments
Project Overview	Dr Susan Smith	Jane Woods	All Stakeholders		E-mail Blast	Program Awareness, why program is being undertaken	
Project Updates	James Dawe	James Dawe	All Stakeholders	Bi-Weekly	E-mail	Update status of project	Targeted messages pre/ during/ post delivery
Project Status	Schedule	James Dawe	Cardiac Staff, Public Affairs, Team Members, Development Office	Weekly	Status meeting	Track status, manage issues	
Kickoff Presentation	Dr. Susan Smith	Jane Woods James Dawe	Cardiac Staff, Public Affairs, Development Office	31 March	Presentation	Project Awareness	Teleconference to include offsite employees

Figure 6.5. Communications matrix for a sponsor dinner.

COMMUNICATIONS MATRIX INSTRUCTIONS	
Field	**Description**
What (Kind of information or event)	Describe the message that needs to go out to this audience, for example "Status Report." Consider the following when defining the message: • What does the project need to communicate? • Who is authoring, sponsoring, and/or "standing behind" the message? • What is going to happen? What other needs or work are related to this? • How far along are we? When is this going to happen? • Where is this going to happen, in what offices? Where is this not going to happen? • How is this going to take place, in what steps or increments? • How will the project team help you get through the change? • What does the recipient need to do, and by what date? • When will there be further communications, follow-ups, etc.? • Where can they get more information? Who should they contact? By when?
Source	• Where is the information coming from? • Who is providing the information? • Does the information need to be confirmed prior to distribution? (If so, by whom?)
By Whom (Stakeholder sending information)	For each message/event in the Communications Matrix identify: • Who will prepare/present the message? • Who will develop the media and coordinate its delivery/presentation? • Who will author or sign the communication? (Who is the message from?)
To Whom (Stakeholders receiving information, who needs to know)	Who is the audience for each communication? Check the Project Charter, Statement of Work and other project documents to determine audiences. Some messages will go to audiences defined by function or group membership: • Project (key project stakeholders, all project personnel, project managers, project sponsors, functional area managers, consultants). • IT (all of IT, key support people, all managers, some managers, direct reports, focus groups, ancillary groups). • User population (users in key groups involved with the project). • Functional Area (functional group participants not on the project team, cross-functional groups, functional group by area group notification). • Corporate (Executive Committee, selected executive officers). • User population (users in key groups involved with the project). Some audiences will be defined by the project stage, milestones, and status: • Introductory audience. • Audience for various stages and milestones. • Implementation audience, by stage. • Conclusion audience for project review and sharing the success.

Figure 6.6. Instructions for completing a communications matrix.

COMMUNICATIONS MATRIX INSTRUCTIONS (continued)	
By When (Frequency or date needed, timing)	Consider the Project Charter stakeholders and the input of project team members and key stakeholders to determine a communication approach and timing.
How (Communication methods/ vehicles)	How to communicate will depend on the stage of the project, the audience, etc. It generally takes face-to-face communication to achieve buy-in support and to get someone to take action. At other times, hard copy print and electronic media or combinations of media are effective. Consider the following: • One-on-one meetings • Group meetings • Letters and other hard copy • Video conferencing • Flyers and pamphlets • E-mail • Telephone (conference calls, etc.)
Why (Purpose of the communication, message objective)	Why is this communication taking place? • What is the intended effect of the communication? • What do we hope to achieve with the communication? • What are the benefits of the communication?
Restrictions	• Are there any information distribution restrictions associated with this information? • Did you consider your contractual obligations for information distribution? • Is this information not intended for publication and/or broad distribution? • Is this information company confidential?
Comments	Add comments as needed to clarify message and/or information distribution requirements. (Update the Project Notebook with modifications.)

Figure 6.6 continued. Instructions for completing a communications matrix.

Address Project Risks

Another area to consider during project planning is the management of *project risks.* The activities associated with identifying a project's risks, analyzing them, and identifying how to react to them should they occur are some of the most important activities you'll undertake.

Your team should assist in identifying potential project risks and possible responses that could be implemented should a risk occur — that is, should it become a true issue for the project. Risk

RISK RESPONSE	EXPLANATION
Mitigate	What can we do to lower the impact the risk will have on our project?
Avoid	What can we do to prevent the risk from happening?
Transfer	Can we ask someone outside the project to address the risk?
Accept	There's nothing we can do about it.

Figure 6.7. Categories of risk response.

responses fall into one of four categories: mitigate, avoid, transfer, or accept (see Figure 6.7).

You, the project sponsor, and your team should collectively determine the most desirable risk response. If that response is likely to impact the project's budget, you should work with the sponsor to ensure that funding will be made available if needed. That tentative funding approval should be documented for future use in case it becomes necessary.

Risk identification and analysis is best accomplished in a workshop setting with full participation by you and the entire project team. It is also beneficial to have subject matter experts participate to share experiences from similar past projects. The workshop should be facilitated by someone not on the project so that you and the project sponsor can participate in the workshop without worrying about the mechanics of running it. During the workshop, participants identify those risks that might occur. Some common risks include:

 GLOSSARY

A *project risk* is an uncertain event that, if it happens, could have an effect (positive or negative) on one or more project objectives.

potential inclement weather for an outside event; failure of a significant donor to provide promised services; insufficient number of volunteers to set up an event.

As each risk is identified, the probability of it happening and the impact it will have on the project should be discussed. All the risks and their mitigation plans should be documented in what is commonly called a risk log (see Figures 6.8 to 6.11). This document should be a "living" document, reviewed and updated as part of the project's management meetings and reviews. A risk log can be used to capture these risks, their probability of occurring, and their impact. When all have been captured, the weighted probability is calculated and the collective team determines what the risk response will be for those risks whose weighted probability exceeds your organization's risk threshold. Your organization's risk threshold is a measure of how much risk your organization is willing to take. It might vary from project to project, depending on the project's overall criticality. So this is a metric to discuss with the project's sponsor. A high number indicates a risk-averse posture, a lower number indicates a willingness to assume certain risks.

With sufficient foresight risks can often be avoided or mitigated. Sometimes that might mean setting aside part of the project's budget to deal with a risk should it occur. For example, the mitigation plan for inclement weather might be moving an event inside; should that be needed, then there might be costs for using a facility or decreasing ticket sales. Or the risk related to inclement weather could be avoided entirely by changing the venue to make it an inside event no matter the weather conditions. The risk associated with not having enough volunteers to set up the event might be mitigated by contracting with a temporary staffing agency or paying staff to work additional hours. When determining risk response, project teams are encouraged to be creative and to really think within the realms of possibility; they shouldn't initially constrain their recommendations. You and the project sponsor can apply the reality constraints (often budget) as needed.

RISK RESPONSE LOG

Purpose	To document the description and assessment of risks and to offer action plans to respond to risks. The Risk Log provides a reference for the project team and supports their need to be apprised of and evaluate the risks. A risk is an uncertain event or condition, which if it occurs, has a positive or negative affect on project objectives. All risks will be listed on the Risk Log, and only those risks with a risk level of 5 or above will be listed on the Detailed Risk Response Form. Do not list all business risks, just list business risks that relate to the current project. .

Project Identification

Project Name				Project Number			Date Created	
Sponsor Dinner							20110301	
Project Sponsor		Project Owner		Project Manager			Program Manager	
Dr. Susan Smith		Jane Woods		James Dawe				

Date Identified	Risk No.	Risk Description	Category	Potential Impact	Risk Owner	Probability Occurrence (1 – 5)	Impact of Risk (1 – 5)	Risk Level (1 – 25)	Response	Status	Date of Invoked Response
03/01/11	1	Lack of response	External Risk	Event does not yield results	Jane Woods	1	5	5	Avoidance		
03/01/11	2	Inclement weather	External Risk	Event does not yield results	James Dawe	2	5	10	Mitigation		
03/01/11	3	Keynote becomes ill and is not able to speak	Technical Risk	Program is limited	Jane Woods	2	4	8	Transference		
03/01/11	4	Insufficient onsite volunteers during event	Resource Risk	Crowds, unhosted tables	James Dawe	3	3	9	Avoidance		

Figure 6.8. Risk response log for a sponsor dinner.

67

RISK RESPONSE LOG INSTRUCTIONS	
Field	**Description**
Date Identified	Use the format mm/dd/yy to list the date the risk was first identified.
Risk No.	List the Risk Number in sequential order, 1, 2, etc.
Risk Description	Describe the risk — an event or condition, which if it occurs, has a positive or negative affect on a project's objectives (e.g., the technology that is being purchased will not be supported by the manufacturer in two months).
Category	Risk Categories are sources of potential risk for classification. Choose the appropriate risk categories: Project Management Risk, Resource Risk, Client Risks, Technical Risks, External Risks, Vendor Risks.
Potential Impact	State how the risk would affect the project if it occurs (e.g., not having manufacturer support for this technology would have an adverse affect on the roll out).
Risk Owner	List the name of the person who has ownership of this risk, and who will make certain the response plan is implemented.
Probability of Occurrence	Indicate the chance that the risk will occur using a scale of 1 – 5, where 1 = low and 5 = high. (Caution: This cell requires that you enter a whole number between 1 and 5.)
Impact of Risk	Indicate the consequence of the risk on the project if it occurs, using a scale of 1 – 5, where 1 = low and 5 = high. (Caution: This cell requires that you enter a whole number between 1 and 5.)
Risk Level	Determine the overall risk level by multiplying the probability of occurrence by the impact of risk. This factor will be automatically computed when using the spreadsheet. If the Risk Level is 16 or above complete the Detailed Risk Response Form.
Response	Choose from one of the following responses. Acceptance: Accept the consequences, will not hurt the overall project success, but may delay a milestone. Avoidance: Eliminate the cause of the risk - change the project direction to protect the project objectives from this impact. Mitigation: Take action to reduce probability that the risk will occur to an acceptable threshold. Transference: Transfer the responsibility of managing the risk, including ownership and acceptance of consequences. Transference does not eliminate the risk.
Status	Choose from the list the status of the risk: New, Under Review, In Progress, Completed.
Date of Invoked Response	Use the format mm/dd/yy to list the date the response strategy was invoked/implemented.

Figure 6.9. Instructions for completing a risk response log.

68

DETAILED RISK RESPONSE LOG

Purpose	This document is used to further define the risks on the Risk Log if needed. The objective is to document and analyze the detailed risk. Not all risks will use this form, only those that are listed on the Risk Log with a risk level of 16 or higher. Risks with a level of 16 or higher represent those with high impact and a high probability of occurring, so trying to prevent the risk and creating a contingency plan would benefit the project.

Project Identification

Project Name		Project Number		Date Created
Sponsor Dinner				20110301

Project Sponsor	Project Owner	Project Manager	Program Manager
Dr. Susan Smith	Jane Woods	James Dawe	

Risk No.	Category	Further Definition of Risk	Loss Hours/Cost	Preventative Risk Hours/Cost	Response	Preventive Strategic Plan	Contingency Strategic Plan
1	External Risk	Insufficient attendance	$20K in lost profits; unknown impact on solicitations	$1.5K for extra marketing department support; $10K in advertising costs	Avoidance	Focus on marketing plans	
2	External Risk	Bad weather impacts attendance	$20K in lost profits; unknown impact on solicitations	40 hours of volunteer time to explore options	Mitigation	Look at alternative locations closer to main roads	
3	Technical Risk	Dr Johnson is a major draw; without him, numbers could be off	$20K in lost profits; unknown impact on solicitations	no costs	Transference	Ask Dr. Johnson to arrange an alternate for us	
4	Resource Risk	Rely on volunteers to act as table hosts to solicit further participation	Unknown impact on solicitations	$25K in printing costs	Avoidance	See if printing solicitation materials to augment table hosts is feasible	

Figure 6.10. Detailed risk response log for a sponsor dinner.

69

DETAILED RISK RESPONSE LOG INSTRUCTIONS	
Field	Description
Risk No.	List the Risk Number on the Risk Log this correlates with.
Category	Typically risks are classified according to their cause, source, or area of impact. Define the category of Risk — Project Management Risk, Resource Risk, Client Risk, Technical Risk, External Risk, Vendor Risk. Choose from the drop down box.
Further Definition of Category	Within the category, further definition may be needed such as software equipment, customer, configuration, logistics, communications, or other.
Loss Hour / Cost	Determine the anticipated number of labor hours or cost that will be lost if the risk occurs.
Preventative Risk Hours / Cost	Establish the anticipated number of hours or cost that it will take to determine and create a preventive strategy or contingency plan.
Response	Choose from one of the responses below. Acceptance: Accept the consequences, will not hurt the overall project success, but may delay a milestone. Avoidance: Eliminate the cause of the risk - change the project direction to protect the project objectives from this impact. Mitigation: Take action to reduce probability that the risk will occur to an acceptable threshold. Transference: Transfer the responsibility of managing the risk, including ownership, and acceptance of consequences. Transference does not eliminate the risk.
Preventive Strategic Plan	Determine what steps will be taken to prevent this risk from occurring. Example: Traveling to a site with a mobile lab with 14 laptops, 250 feet of cable, 2 hubs, and 1 server. The Ethernet cards in the laptops could possibly be damaged in the shipping process. To try to prevent this from occurring, special packaging will be used to ship the mobile lab.
Contingency Strategic Plan	List the backup plan that will be implemented if the risk event actually occurs. Example: The person traveling will carry two additional Ethernet cards. In each city, a vendor has been researched and contacted prior to deployment in that city to make sure laptop inventory is available if needed.

Figure 6.11. instructions for completing a detailed risk response log.

Plan Some More!

Planning sets the stage upon which the project will be executed. And while planning needs to occur at the beginning of the project, a superior project manager (that's you) never finishes planning. Planning and re-planning are continuous throughout the life of the project as events occur that impact the project's budget, resources, or scope. As you receive status updates, you should review the project's schedule, budget, risk, and resource plans to determine if something needs to be modified to ensure that the project continues to stay on track. You should also stay abreast with the happenings in the community in which your project is occurring. If a new organization is announced, if a significant new need is identified by your board of directors, if a competing event is announced — these are all activities that are external to your project but could have an impact on the project's overall success. Their impact should be assessed and addressed with your project sponsor to determine if a response is required. We can all think of projects we've undertaken that were impacted, both negatively and positively, by external events.

Case Study: Project Planning

Recently I was approached by the special events planner from our local healthcare system's trust to serve as a chairperson for an upcoming event. A new chair was being sought because the former chair had relocated from the region and none of the former team members were interested in the position. I was new to the event being planned but had an affiliation with the specific organization it was supporting, so I willingly took on the assignment.

One of the goals of the assignment, as explained to me by the event planner, was to introduce some new concepts, new practices, and new team members to the team to replace team members who were expressing interest in other volunteer roles. There was also a desire on the part of the trust to increase the revenue produced by the event.

One of the first steps I took with the project team, after my introduction and participation in the kickoff meeting that the event planner facilitated, was to ask one of the returning team members to be my deputy to provide some continuity in the leadership decisions that were to be made. It also permitted me to "divide and conquer" what would turn out to be an intensive sprint of six month's effort over the holiday season. I then arranged for the event planner to meet with me and my deputy, to establish the project life cycle model and the initial work breakdown structure. This permitted us to make assignments to ourselves to do more detailed planning with the existing team members. This more detailed planning started with reviewing that work breakdown structure with the team, soliciting support and leadership for each of the major work packages. Each team member then reviewed their required activities and identified "complete by" dates that the event planner pulled into a milestone schedule, which she used to track progress.

My deputy and I also met with the event planner to review the project's budget and to ensure that funds had been allocated to each of the work packages that required them. We used this session to also identify where sponsorships or in-kind services would be beneficial. This list was then provided to the team members working these focus areas, in coordination with the trust's staff. Volunteers and staff collectively experienced tremendous success in obtaining the community support.

The event planner met offline with the trust's public affairs department to synchronize our event's schedule for graphic and marketing support. She also met with the organization's mailing department to coordinate our dates for anticipated mailings. The milestone schedule we had produced was very beneficial in both these discussions in that it permitted her to assess and communicate the impact that delays in those dates would have on the event.

At this point, with our schedule, budget, and resource assignments well in hand, the team turned its attention to risk identification and analysis: what had gone wrong in the past, what could go wrong this time, and how could we mitigate or respond if it did happen? Our event was scheduled during the time of year when adverse weather was a definite risk to be considered. Our preferred mitigation plan was to ensure that an alternative date was indeed viable and to let ticket purchasers know of that date. Another risk was the lack of a sufficient number of "day of event" volunteers. We mitigated that risk by offering compensatory event attendance for those volunteers as well as arranging with our site vendor to have paid staff on hand as supplements.

The biggest risk we faced, however, was insufficient participation overall. We attempted to mitigate any chance of this risk occurring by focusing attention on the event's marketing campaign. My deputy was successful in leveraging her professional connections to obtain some visible participants, including several popular restaurants to provide some renowned hors d'oeuvres. The trust provided a heartfelt, touching case study to feature in the marketing materials and in a talk presented during the event. And one of the local sponsors provided a particularly enticing piece of jewelry to be raffled during the event. We were also able to secure numerous donations of goods and services, enabling us to continue providing popular onsite silent auction tables, to supplement the core event.

The event that year was the most profitable and least issue-plagued as a result of this upfront planning and pro-active management of potential issues. The use of management practices such as meeting agendas and meeting minutes distributed in advance, the use of meeting time to work on issues as opposed to status reporting, and the delegation of responsibility to team members were some of the practices introduced that continue to be used today.

Summary

Taking the time to adequately think about the project, the activities and effort it will require, the resources available, how communications will occur, and what your project team's response would be should a risk occur, is a critical success factor for a project. Yet time and time again a project team starts running the race without thinking about the course, often in response to unstated expectations of project stakeholders. It's important for the project manager and project sponsor to insist that time be provided for the team to do the necessary planning and to ensure that project details are identified and understood before starting the project.

7

Becoming an Agile Nonprofit

With the emergence and acceptance of the Internet and its associated technology since the late 20th century, we are truly approaching the state of a single global society and a single global economy or, as Thomas Friedman calls it, "a flattened world." This shift has had an impact on how businesses interact with and support nonprofit organizations. The days of the multi-year commitment are dwindling as businesses and individuals realize the economic impact of this dynamic global environment. Consequently, the boards and managers of nonprofits need to be ready to respond with tools and techniques such as agile project management.

There is also a growing recognition that today's business workers, including those supporting our nonprofits, are knowledge workers, with a sense of empowerment and a need to be involved in making the decisions that affect their workday and their volunteer efforts. They want their management to be leaders, to set the vision and establish simple rules, and to let the team adapt as needed to achieve that vision.

What Does It Mean to Be Agile?

There is much being written these days about the need for agility in today's businesses, especially in projects related to the development of *strategic differentiators,* such as a new medical facility or dormitory. Yet, it's not clear that there's a true understanding or appreciation for what's meant by the term agility. To the dismay of some managers, agility does not mean unmanaged or undocumented. Rather, agility means the ability to quickly adjust and respond to changing business needs. It means achieving goals before the loss of a donor's attention or commitment.

 GLOSSARY

Strategic differentiators **are those projects that result in outcomes that differentiate the non-profit in the marketplace, such as the capital campaign that funds the development of a cancer center within a healthcare system.**

It means being responsive at the local and global level to immediate needs. It means that "do more with less" now translates into "achieve it faster," whatever "it" is.

Agile project management reflects the ability to apply just enough of the project management practices to ensure that the business objectives for the project are achieved. This usually translates into just enough planning to know that the budget is sufficient, to identify the risks likely to occur and what the team will do when they occur, to determine who has what decision-making authorities, and to know how information about the project, especially project status, will be communicated.

Agile project management is not for the inexperienced project manager, but if you work at it you'll find that you become more agile with every project you manage. It relies as much on the ability of the project manager to read individuals, to make quick decisions when needed, and to know when to let the team take the lead and when the team requires specific direction. Agile project management is more about active leadership than about bureaucratic management.

KEY CONCEPTS OF AGILE PROJECT MANAGEMENT

- Active leadership
- Close interaction between the project sponsor and the project team
- Less time dedicated to planning at the beginning of the project
- Smaller teams and more highly skilled team members
- Delayed decision making
- Elimination of waste
- Integrated quality activities

Figure 7.1. Agile project management is based on the concepts above. Agile nonprofits demonstrate the ability to quickly adjust and respond to changing business needs while managing their projects.

Acknowledge Dynamics and Change

Project sponsors frequently do not dig deeply enough into resolving an important issue — that is, they don't sort out the difference between "wants" and "needs." Only after the project starts does the sponsor begin to realize that what the organization really needs may not be exactly what they requested. That's why you need an approach to project management that allows you to deal with the reality of change. You need to be able to break down the final, long-term objective (which is subject to change) into a series of near-term objectives (which are less likely to change), incorporating discovery and learning throughout the project life cycle.

By applying agile project management you actively work with your sponsor throughout the project life cycle. You jointly make adjustments and even redirect the project by using an iterative approach to managing the project, an approach that deals with the level of uncertainty that you encounter. You use agile techniques to supplement the traditional project management practices that you already use (see Figure 7.1).

Use Basic Common Agile Practices

Agile project management is all about sharing the ownership of a project vision and then influencing, motivating, and enabling others to be successful. As project managers, the contributions you'll make in an agile project are more akin to those of a team leader or facilitator than a manager. With an increased emphasis on the team (which includes the project's customers), your role becomes one of "roadblock removal," while the self-managing team generates the necessary information to move the project forward and makes decisions based on that information.

There are a number of techniques that can be used to help your project team be agile. Figure 7.2 highlights a few that I've found to be practical when working with a team consisting of staff and volunteers.

Agile project management calls for more leadership … and less dictatorship. In an article published in the Harvard Business School's weekly newsletter, Maggie Starvish observed that "fluid project teams" are needed in today's businesses. She notes that "stable teams that plan first and execute later are increasingly infeasible in the twenty-first century workforce." She further points out that there's an increasing need for strong interpersonal processes that enable individuals to rapidly come together to accomplish a common objective in ever-decreasing time frames.

An example of the good use of agile project management was the volunteer response to the relief needs resulting from Hurricane Sandy. Those response teams didn't have time for elaborate planning, role definition, or budget development. They needed to quickly determine who could do what and when, and then get going at responding. Small teams were fielded to various neighborhoods, each with a focused assignment and an expectation of quick completion of the immediate task, with further recovery to be addressed by another team at a later date.

At the same time, the initial response teams needed to establish communications that enabled the public, including news reporters,

TECHNIQUES FOR MANAGING YOUR PROJECTS WITH AGILITY	
Technique	Description
Project Wall Board	Establish a bulletin board in a location accessible to all team members; post status reports, meeting minutes, and other pieces of information to it. If a physical bulletin board is not practical, consider establishing a SharePoint site or a similar repository, bearing in mind that some volunteers might not have ready access to it.
Daily Stand-Up Meetings	These are particularly useful when approaching a key deliverable or date. Research shows that meeting participants stay focused and meetings are expedited if participants remain standing and if only those participants who are needed to give an update are present. Hold these meetings in front of your Project Wall Board whenever possible so that you can manually update the status reports on it. If volunteers are to be part of the meetings, then add a teleconference line so that they can call in to the meeting. After the meeting, remove the marked-up status reports and generate a new report reflective of the meeting so that non-attendees can read what transpired.
Repeatable Templates	Provide your project team with templates for information you wish to receive from them periodically, such as status reports and lessons learned reports. This will enable you to more easily consolidate their information.
Project Notebook	Maintain 3-ring physical binders for all project information. This will protect you against any lack of access to your electronic files in addition to ensuring that a comprehensive project history is available for the next time a project of a similar nature is undertaken. I have found it useful to have one binder that contains the Project Management Plan with the latest schedule, risk log, and budget reports, and then a separate binder that contains copies of all important project communications and e-mails, especially those that document a decision, commitment, or authorization. These binders accompanied me to any project meeting I attended. If the latter binder became too bulky, I would create a third binder containing only the last month's communications.

Figure 7.2. Some project management techniques to help you be more agile.

to know what needs were being addressed, which ones remained, and how assistance could be rendered. Many of these organizations turned very quickly to social media and smartphones to enable those communications.

Any safety measures that needed to be considered in the activities associated with the relief efforts were quickly identified and integrated into the responses — building inspectors, firemen, and other safety officials worked side-by-side with the responders to ensure that safety aspects were addressed.

Contrast these relief efforts with those following the 2010 earthquake in Haiti, where relief efforts are still grossly incomplete years later. Those relief efforts were managed with a less agile approach, reflective of the complex multi-national response the disaster invoked.

Summary

Change happens more often and more quickly in today's world. Nonprofits have to be able to adapt quickly to that change in order to achieve their mission. Whether responding rapidly to a crisis or being prepared for the unexpected, agile nonprofits apply just enough project management to ensure that the project's objectives are achieved.

8

The Superior
Project Manager

Those highly experienced in using project management practices agree that the project manager is the single most important factor impacting project goal achievement. This individual is assigned the responsibilities of planning, scheduling, and orchestrating the day-to-day tasks required to achieve the project's objectives. In some instances the project manager has direct authority over the staff assigned to the project, but in many instances the project manager must rely on the efforts of staff from other departments or on volunteers in order to achieve project success. This requires leadership skills.

As I've demonstrated in the preceding chapters, project management is a unique profession, with a known set of competencies and required technical knowledge, and it's not a profession for everyone. That is, many people will try project management; some will succeed, some will not. Some organizations administer competency assessments to determine who among the staff or volunteers has the ability to succeed in a project manager role. These assessments typically measure the candidate in three core areas: knowledge, potential, and behavior.

There are basic skills and personal qualities that project managers need in order to be consistently successful in managing projects. You may already have these skills and qualities. If so, you'll be a superior project manager from the start. If not, you'll want to make an effort to learn these skills, to develop these qualities, so that in time you'll become a superior project manager. After all, some of your projects may be critical to meeting your nonprofit's goals, maybe even saving lives.

Be an Active Leader

Active leadership skills are the most important abilities all superior project managers possess. After all, project managers are often responsible for overseeing multiple projects simultaneously, using staff over which they have no direct authority, delegating tasks to them, and working with them to achieve a number of various objectives. Leadership gurus talk about two kinds of leadership: passive and active; the best project managers demonstrate the latter.

Passive leaders allow their team members to do the work independently and provide little guidance as to how they want activities completed. Passive leaders are reactive; they wait until asked to provide assistance or to address an issue. Sometimes this hesitancy might be related to wanting to permit team members to resolve an issue by themselves, and sometimes it might be related to uncertainty as to how to proceed. At other times it might be related to not wanting to upset someone, to wanting to be "nice" to everyone associated with the project.

Active leaders, on the other hand, exhibit a take-charge attitude, a willingness to engage with the project team to solve issues, to take on challenges, and to see activities to completion, even if it means upsetting the apple cart. You need to be an active leader.

As an active leader you need to be fully engaged with your team. You must be willing to communicate the hard decisions that need to be made, make them, and be proactive in resolving issues.

SKILLS AND ATTRIBUTES OF A SUPERIOR PROJECT MANAGER

A project manager needs to be:

■ An active leader	■ Technologically savvy
■ Efficient	■ Results-focused
■ A good communicator	■ Intelligent
■ Decisive	■ Confident
■ Honest	■ Skilled at technical project management

Figure 8.1. These are the basic skills and attributes that project managers need in order to be consistently successful in managing projects.

Active leaders are road block removers — the people who see the brick wall that their team is approaching and who initiate action to ensure that the wall is out of the way by the time their team gets there. As an active leader you'll need two sets of eyes — one set focused on the road ahead for each project, the other set focused on the team you're leading.

As an active leader you'll lead your project team daily. You'll review the project plan, foreseeing needed activities and initiating those activities, at the right time. Rather than taking on specific activities yourself, you'll encourage team members to complete the required project work, thereby maintaining your ability to perform crucial activities associated with decision making, communications, risk management, and oversight of the project's budget, while being available to assist team members whenever called upon.

This kind of project leadership competence is not learned in school. Rather it's developed over time, through prior work experience, and is enhanced by formal awareness training and mentoring. When asked about famous leaders, leaders who stand out in their minds, many individuals cite former military officers, recognizing that the training and experience these individuals received during their military careers made them effective leaders.

Be Efficient

You need to be efficient. Superior project managers are the ultimate task jugglers, able to shift direction when the situation requires. They're diligent in ensuring that the project team works efficiently to complete only what's necessary to deliver projects on time, within budget, and without sacrificing quality. They encourage their project team to take the fewest possible steps to get things done. They follow the simplest possible methodologies, standards, procedures, and templates, aligning the application of these tools to the requirements and risk profile of the project at hand. If there is a corporate-mandated process that doesn't seem to be necessary for the project's success, the superior project manager will tactfully question the process and attempt to obtain a waiver rather than blindly adhere to the process.

 QUICK TIP

If your team consists of mostly volunteers, it's not wise to schedule meetings in the morning.

Along with efficiency you'll need good prioritization, time management, and organization skills. Superior project managers know what to do, when to do it, and in which order to complete tasks. They understand which meetings are crucial to the project's success and which ones are not necessary. They are effective in managing their in-box rather than letting their in-box manage them. As a superior project manager you'll understand your energy cycle and the energy cycle of your team, and you'll employ it when planning their work day and work week, scheduling activities accordingly.

Be a Good Communicator

To be a superior project manager you'll need to have effective communication skills in order to clearly delegate responsibilities and give instructions to your project team. And because you'll serve as the liaison between your project team and your executives, good communication skills will be critically important. In these days of instant messages, e-mails and tweets, it's important to realize that you cannot easily retract what you send. One lesson I've learned is to use my draft folder. When I've finished writing a message, be it an e-mail or an instant message, I save it for a couple of hours. Then, before I send it, I read it again with a fresh viewpoint to make sure it says what I want it to say in a manner that's clear and concise, with no hidden messages in the words. I also check for spelling and grammatical errors.

Remember that communication skills include listening skills. Do not hesitate to apply the "Right now is not a good time to talk" rule if someone is trying to discuss something with you when you are distracted by another matter. Instead, make an appointment to talk with the individual as soon as you are available, and then keep that appointment. I have found it useful to take three deep breaths before answering the phone, to clear my head and to put a "smile on my face" that will come across in the manner in which I answer the phone. You need to know when to speak, when to listen, and how to resolve issues and conflicts in a calm and professional manner.

Be Decisive

As a project manager you'll be asked on a daily basis to quickly make critical decisions to keep your project moving forward. You may not always have time to research all the options or to explore all risks regarding your project. So in order to make critical decisions, you'll need to exercise critical thinking skills — that is, think through the decision in a manner that's clear, rational, open-minded, and informed by evidence. Many times you'll need to trust in past similar experiences or solicit guidance from others before making decisions. Regardless, the decision is yours to make and you can't hesitate to take ownership and make it.

Be Honest

Project managers are role models for the entire project team. Therefore you must conduct yourself honestly and ethically in order to instill a sense of confidence, pride, loyalty, and trust throughout your project team. Don't hesitate to promptly share information with your project team. It's better for them to hear news, good or bad, from you than from any grapevine or informal communications. One of the worst experiences I had as a volunteer was learning in a newspaper article that the conference on which I was working was cancelled. Our project manager had been trying to schedule a group meeting in which to inform us, but in the meantime, the project sponsor shared the news with a local reporter.

Likewise, encourage open and honest interactions between project team members. Trust them to be honest with each other as to status of activities and issues they're facing. Empower your team to communicate directly with each other, keeping you apprised of outcomes and decisions. Don't insist that you be copied on all communications; that will send a message of distrust. Determine which communications are important, which decisions are critical, and ask to be involved in those matters only. By creating a project management culture that promotes honesty and trustworthiness, your organization will experience greater efficiencies, fewer risks, decreased costs, and improved profitability.

Be Technologically Savvy

In today's fast-moving, technology-driven, global nonprofit environments, collaboration tools are necessary to bring together project teams that are geographically disbursed and in different time zones. You'll need to be able to build high-performing project teams with people who are not co-located through the efficient and effective use of project management support tools — scheduling tools such as Microsoft Project or Project Central; document sharing tools such as Microsoft SharePoint; e-mail and calendar tools such as Microsoft Outlook; virtual meeting tools such as Wiggio; and communications tools such as Twitter and Facebook, about which we will talk in further detail in Chapter 9. The appropriate use of these tools will enhance the agility of your project, by minimizing the effort associated with administering the project — be it project communications, schedules, or budgets.

If you're not familiar with a particular tool or technology, ask your team members if any of them have had experience with the tool and if they would be willing to share that knowledge with the team. If no one has, you might ask the organization's IT department for assistance. And if you still aren't able to find someone, then you might ask the organization's volunteer manager to search among all volunteers to see if there's someone in the volunteer pool. If all else fails, locate a local training partner who might be willing to provide the training as an in-kind service to the organization, including you.

Be Results-Focused

Ongoing behavioral studies make it clear that ambition is an important factor in business goal achievement. But you must be careful that your ambition doesn't make you ruthless or selfish. You must use your determination to accomplish goals for the organization as a whole and for your project, rather than for your own personal gain. A results-focused project manager keeps the overall project objectives in mind when making decisions. When making decisions for the project, be sure you're making decisions that are the best for project performance, not for the benefit of a particular sponsor or donor or team member. This might be difficult when a donor offers the use of his restaurant for an event, but you know that restaurant is not in a desirable location, which will detract from overall ticket sales. You need to determine if the economic benefits of using that particular restaurant outweigh the loss in ticket revenue before replying to the offer.

Be Intelligent

As a superior project manager you'll need to possess strong analytical skills to be able to understand the status of the project and the implications of requested changes. You'll also need good judgment and strategic thinking skills to be able to make sound decisions even under uncertain circumstances. These qualities are more important to project management achievement than natural intelligence. In addition, superior project managers acknowledge the limits of their knowledge and know who in their organization possesses the needed knowledge.

☑ QUICK TIP

If possible, hold your team meetings on-site at the nonprofit, so the team members can obtain a feel for the nonprofit. Arrange for the team to have a tour of the facility. Consider having a guest speaker at some of your meetings, someone who will benefit from the project's outcome.

It's especially useful for the project manager to be knowledgeable about the particular nonprofit being supported. If you're being asked to lead a walk-a-thon in support of a food bank, your first-hand knowledge of how the food bank operates will enable you to better communicate the project's objectives to a potential volunteer, to motivate a sponsor to make a donation, to keep your project team's enthusiasm high. Share your knowledge with your team. When you're communicating to them a change in direction for the project, explain why. Encourage them to ask questions, and if you don't have the answers, say so, and then obtain and distribute the answers in a timely fashion.

Be Confident

Project managers who are confident in their decisions are most likely to succeed. These leaders believe that their project outcomes are the result of their decisions and actions and are not due to luck, fate, or chance.

As a confident leader you must also have confidence in your project team's ability and must openly demonstrate that confidence. Think of yourself as the team's coach — cheer them on in achieving the project's objectives. Celebrate with them as milestones are achieved. Be supportive of your team members and provide assistance when it's needed, expressing your confidence in their ability to perform. Champion them when outsiders question their abilities. If you have doubts, share them with a peer outside the project; solicit inputs on a confidential basis. Never let your team hear you express doubt in their ability to achieve a milestone or a project's objectives.

Be Skilled at Technical Project Management

Even with the right personal and professional attributes, you need to be knowledgeable in the language and concepts of project management to be successful. Superior project managers display a high degree of expertise in adapting structured project management methodologies and procedures to fit the needs of their projects. They know the value of a project risk review, when it's important to engage the entire project team in such a review, and when such a review can be conducted with just a few team representatives. They understand how a communications matrix can be leveraged to ensure stakeholders are kept apprised of the project activities and status, without those communications becoming a project unto itself. Above all else, superior project managers know when a project is getting out of control and when to ask for assistance.

Summary

What does it take to be a successful project manager? How can you and your manager determine if the project manager role is right for you?

Superior project managers are not necessarily the technical stars on the project team. Rather they are the leaders who pull the team together and keep it focused on achieving the project's objectives. It's the possession of certain character attributes and the ability to supply leadership that differentiate the so-so project managers from the ones who are truly superior.

9

Using Technology in Your Nonprofit Projects

Let's face it — technology is pervasive. Almost every household has at least one computer and one cellphone. The use of social media such as Facebook, Twitter, and LinkedIn has become commonplace in business. Many people under 50 years old send text messages as frequently as they place phone calls. And the use of e-mail and on-line transactions has had such an impact on traditional mail that the U.S. Postal Service has seen a drastic drop in the number of pieces of mail it handles.

Social Media and Your Nonprofit

This expansion in the use of technology provides your nonprofit with an additional toolset in its planning and management of projects. In fact, technology allows you to undertake activities never before possible. For instance, one nonprofit, Operation NH Cares, started off as just a Facebook page established to request assistance for victims of Hurricane Sandy in 2012. The creator of that page received such an overwhelming response that she established a virtual nonprofit that allowed the respondents to make tax-deductible donations in support of the victims.

Other nonprofits have established Facebook pages and LinkedIn groups to support project team collaboration and public awareness. Many hospitals have community pages on Facebook, supporting community awareness of hospital events and dissemination of health information such as how to respond to a flu epidemic.

The use of social media to communicate within a project team, with the project's stakeholders, and with the community at large is something to be considered and decided upon by the team and the project sponsor. For example, one project team used Facebook to support communications within a Relay For Life team. The team captain established a group page for her team after determining that all team members were comfortable using Facebook. This page was then used to communicate within the project team. Each member of the team was able to post messages on the team page for all team members to see. They could also send private messages to certain team members. The team captain was able to obtain status reports on the Facebook page via attached files. And the project's communications history was there by virtue of the Facebook page — a page that could be easily printed for archival purposes.

Should the team determine that the use of Facebook or Twitter or LinkedIn would be beneficial, they then need to consider the security of the information being shared and ensure that their communications will be adequately protected. All of these tools, as well as other social media tools, contain a number of security features such as closed groups, that permit the project manager to limit access to the site and its contents.

Check out Figure 9.1 for ideas on ways to use social media to engage your volunteers and manage your projects.

The Mobile Society

In addition to considering how social media can help your nonprofit meet its objectives, you need to consider how the "mobile

SOCIAL MEDIA TACTICS FOR NONPROFITS

Blogs

Use for communicating with many people; you can limit access to a blog to just your team.

■ Use as a project notebook or a shared project log; archive your project documentation.

■ Keep team members updated on important information, such as delays, change requests, additional funding, or deadline extensions.

■ Recognize and reward team member performance.

■ Engage with potential donors and volunteers — remind them of the vital role they can have in their community.

■ Tell stories and build an emotional connection with your community.

Twitter

Use for light touch contact with many people — good for fast and regular updates.

■ Employ to help build your team, keep in contact, and coordinate team activities.

■ Keep your stakeholders informed about project status.

■ Use for your social cause advertising campaigns.

■ Report directly from volunteer events about all the exciting happenings.

■ Tweet links to your donation landing page (be sure to let your followers know how their donation makes a difference).

LinkedIn

Use for building a community; you can limit access to just your team (LinkedIn Groups).

■ Use to support collaboration among your project team members.

■ Connect with other project managers and nonprofit professionals to help you with your efforts.

■ Share information about your events with your connections and post on the LinkedIn Events page.

■ Set up a LinkedIn company page — post status updates, share news, find volunteers, and stay in touch with your followers.

■ Use the LinkedIn application Projects & Teamspaces to schedule meetings, create tasks, track project progress, and more.

Figure 9.1. Ways nonprofits can use social media to help with their projects.

Facebook

Most useful for telling stories and inviting others to share their stories; you can limit access to just your team with Facebook Groups.

- Use Facebook to build more personal relationships with your virtual team — get to know them better, what they're passionate about, and see what they look like.

- Recruit volunteers — get your audience thinking about what they can do to help.

- Create public awareness of the issues and challenges that you face.

- Create a Facebook persona that represents your organization and builds your brand.

- Use Facebook Groups to share documents, make changes and track them, organize meetings, have online group chat sessions.

Wikis

Most useful for sharing information with many people or a group; anyone can contribute content; you can limit access to just your team.

- Use as a searchable central repository of project documents — ideal for small projects.

- Any team member can view, edit, or update documents — great for collaborating or brainstorming.

- Wiki pages are free-form and a good way to track project status.

- Share project information easily with stakeholders and others in your community.

- Keeping meeting minutes, planning your agenda, and brainstorming ideas are good activities to start in using a wiki.

Google Sites

Use to create project-specific websites.

- Create task lists, issue lists, risk lists.

- Use as a central repository of all your important project documents.

- Use calendar to identify deliverable dates.

- Brainstorm ideas.

- Identify what needs to be done, who's going to be doing what, and when things are going to be delivered.

Figure 9.1 continued. Ways to use social media in nonprofits.

YouTube and Pinterest
Use these visually appealing tools primarily for videos, photos, and images.

- Use photos and videos of your events to show off your hard work.

- Sign up for the YouTube Nonprofit Program — call-to-action feature helps you recruit volunteers, solicit donations, and encourage any other actions you want members of your community to take.

- Engage and interact with the YouTube community — allow people to post video comments and have a dialogue.

- Create pin boards on Pinterest with images and videos that relate to your cause — capture the essence of your organization to build a community of potential donors and volunteers.

- Use Pinterest to build team camaraderie — post photos of the project, volunteers at work, results of the project.

All Social Media Channels
Educate your audience about your organization, its mission, and how they can make a difference.

- Invite your followers to your events, and post after the events touting their success.

- Let your community know what you're working on (especially with photos and video) — they'll see that you're actively contributing to the greater good and that working with teammates can be fun; they may even offer to help.

- Share links to information about your volunteer opportunities.

- Use surveys to gather information about your community — who they are, what their interests are, what they think you should be doing.

- Approach stakeholders and encourage them to take deeper actions.

- Encourage stakeholders to write about your organization or its issues and share with others.

- Share the history of your organization — it shows that you've been contributing to society and personalizes your organization.

- Monitor what stakeholders are saying about your organization, your issue, or your programs and use that information to guide your marketing plans.

Figure 9.1 continued. Ways to use social media in nonprofits.

society" is integrated into your world. As stated earlier, most house-holds now have computers and cellphones, and many have adopted smartphones and tablets as communication devices. These devices provide you with additional platforms for disseminating informa-tion and engaging with your volunteer and staff project teams, in a 24/7 environment if desired.

These additional communications pathways are particularly popular with the "millennial generation" — that is, those members of society who were born in the 21st century. These individuals have grown up with multi-media, are very comfortable with the use of mobile technology, and expect it to be used in their careers and social interactions. You need to engage this generation in the way they want to be engaged. Their attention is grabbed by interac-tive media in the form of podcasts and short videos on YouTube, not by flyers or printed newsletters sent via traditional mail. Don't rely on old-school marketing to reach this community. You need to be agile — don't let information get stale or become yesterday's post. Be concise, be nimble, be proactive — anticipate this genera-tion's needs.

Summary

Your nonprofit needs to acknowledge the many new communica-tion channels and be strategic in how it leverages new technology in its fundraising approaches. You need to plan for the safe and secure adoption of online fundraising. You also need to leverage new technology to engage with your community, especially volun-teers and potential volunteers. Embrace social media and mobile technology. But remember to establish guidelines for the secure use of these tools in all fundraising projects and volunteer efforts.

PART THREE

Volunteer Management in Project-Based Nonprofits

10

Managing Volunteers

Volunteers, like paid employees, require a certain amount of guidance and support in order to achieve success and to have a rewarding experience supporting your organization. That support needs to start before you recruit; you need to think about the kind of volunteers your project will require, when you'll need them, and how you'll integrate them into your existing organizational structure.

Identify the Need for Volunteers

Volunteer management in *project-based nonprofits* begins with identifying where volunteers are needed and where they can make the most impact. In Chapter 6, I introduced the concept of the work breakdown structure and how it can be used to identify volunteer opportunities. Each identified activity within the structure represents work to be performed, either by a staff member or a volunteer. You can use this list of activities to determine the number of volunteers needed as well as the skills those volunteers should possess and when those volunteers will be needed. This determination will ensure that the volunteers are assigned to work when needed and to tasks aligned with their individual skills.

To accomplish this determination, you should first conduct a position analysis. You should review the activities within the work breakdown structure, grouping them into logical positions, and develop position descriptions, just as a department manager would do when establishing a new job within a department. A volunteer position description (see Figure 10.1) should be similar to a job description that's used for employees, with a few caveats.

 GLOSSARY

Project-based nonprofits are nonprofit organizations that operate through projects. Such projects could include, but are not limited to, fundraising events, campaigns, direct mail, appeals and donor recognition events.

First, most states have regulations covering the use of non-paid personnel. You or the individual creating these volunteer position descriptions should consult your legal advisor to ensure compliance with the regulations. For instance, it might be that rather than calling the documents being created "position descriptions" you might call them "committee roles and responsibilities" so that there is no confusion as to the intent. One nonprofit organization with which I worked developed these committee roles and responsibilities documents and made them available to their volunteers via a website that was clearly marked for volunteers so that there was no confusion about the positions not being employment positions.

Another area of caution is the type and amount of activity the volunteer is to perform. Again, states have regulations that limit the number of hours a volunteer can work and the type of work for which they can be used. It's possible that you can use a volunteer to stuff envelopes in support of an event, but you need to be sure that you're not using a volunteer to perform that task just so that you can terminate a paid position.

Each volunteer position description should contain explicit language relative to performance requirements. If you know from past

LOGISTICS CHAIR ROLES AND RESPONSIBILITIES

Specific Responsibilities

- Receives training/orientation from chair and/or staff partner
- Reviews Leadership Handbook
- Recruits subcommittee members including onsite volunteers before and after event
- Participates in all committee meetings except as excused by Committee Chair
- Provides timely and accurate status and budget report updates to Committee Chair
- Requests authorization to use facility rent-free and secures paperwork
- Arranges for all material needs (tables, chairs, flatbed, tents, etc.)
- Walks through location for exact placement of logistical support, medical, committee headquarters, etc.
- Arranges restroom and shower facilities, sound system, and lighting if needed
- Arranges first-aid station and setup, and recruits necessary medical personnel
- Sets up water stations
- Transports material and sets up site on the day of the event

General Responsibilities

- Performs all functions in a cheerful and cooperative professional manner
- Is physically present and accessible before, during, and after the event
- Makes arrangements for appropriate representation if unable to attend committee meetings
- Treats all volunteer and staff personnel with respect and dignity
- Responds to all inquiries and requests within 48 hours of request

Position Requirements

- Attention to detail
- Good judgment and decision-making skills
- Able to make decisions under pressure
- Good communications skills
- Demonstrated team-player
- Able to attend monthly evening committee meetings and commit to event participation
- Anticipated volunteer period: October 2011 through December 2012

Figure 10.1. Volunteer position description.

experience that physical attendance in monthly committee meetings is needed, then state that in the position description. If there's an expectation that the volunteers will attend the event they're working on, then state that fact and tell the volunteers whether scholarships or grants are available to assist with fees. Another requirement that should be clearly identified is what time of day the volunteers will be needed to work. For instance, volunteers supporting solicitation of sponsorships or in-kind services should understand that some amount of their volunteer efforts will be needed during business hours. However, I've found that information is not always made clear to prospective volunteers, which can lead to problems later. Volunteers will be unhappy when they're asked to perform tasks or attend meetings that they were unaware were required, and projects won't have the volunteer support they need.

Another requirement you need to make clear in the position description is whether the volunteer needs to be proficient with technology and, if so, what technology. As I previously mentioned, many younger volunteers will prefer text messages to phone conversations, e-mail to letters. However, there is still a segment of volunteers who don't have ready access to the Internet in their homes or don't carry smartphones. If these communication vehicles will be needed to support the project, then state so in the position description. Also, identify whether the organization can provide the technology if needed.

Establish the Project Team's Structure

In addition to defining the positions for which volunteers will be recruited, you'll need to consider how the committee or project team will be organized. Project teams, or volunteer committees, require structure to ensure that the needed work is performed within the determined budget and schedule and that the stakeholders are kept apprised of progress. Structure is also needed to ensure that no duplication of effort occurs. Establishing a committee structure is as much about the synergies within the committee as it is about reporting. As you review the position descriptions you've developed, consider how the different roles depend on and interact with each other. Close interaction might indicate that a sub-committee could be beneficial.

Many organizations default to a very broad, flat structure, with all volunteers reporting directly to the project manager. While this might be desirable for control purposes, it often becomes unwieldy, especially if you're a staff member with other responsibilities. The more successful projects with which I've been involved, including an all-volunteer-managed international conference with over 3,000 attendees, chose a different structure. I call this structure the "satellite organization." Figure 10.2 depicts this structure, in which there's a core committee that reports directly to the project manager, with sub-committees supporting key areas of responsibility. Each sub-committee has a charter that addresses the sub-committee's authority and autonomy. Each member of the core team is a sub-committee chair, with volunteers working on the activities in their specific area of responsibility. They hold their own committee meetings, where details within their realm of authority are addressed. The sub-committee chair reports back to the core committee on items that impact budget, schedule, or overall theme and provides status updates on the work of the sub-committee.

This structure is ideal in that it:

- Addresses logistical challenges that can arise with a large committee

- Provides volunteers with opportunities to be leaders

- Enables the project manager to truly focus on the overall project.

I highly recommend this structure if the number of volunteers working on the project exceeds five or six.

In addition to contemplating committee organization, you or the committee chair must understand to whom you'll be report-

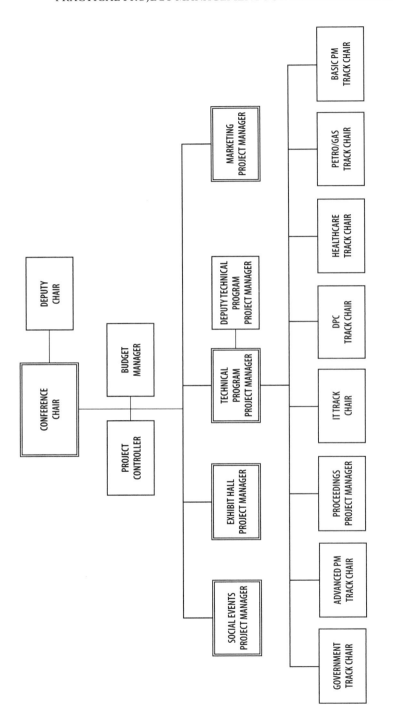

Figure 10.2. Satellite/project team organization chart for a special event. Each member of this core team is a sub-committee chair, with volunteers working on the activities in their specific area of responsibility. I recommend this structure if the number of volunteers working on the project exceeds five or six.

ing. Will it be to a staff member or will it be directly to the project sponsor (typically a board member)? How frequently will that interaction occur, and with what degree of formality? In Chapter 6 I talked about developing a communications plan for the project. One of the entries in that plan should address this interaction between the committee chair and whomever the chair reports to.

Staff Your Project Team

Now that you have your organizational structure, and you know to whom you're reporting, you can start to recruit to fill volunteer positions, especially those that are needed early in the project's schedule. This is so important an undertaking that Chapter 12 is dedicated to the topic. However, one key point to bear in mind is that you need to recruit with the same discipline you would for a paying position. You are entrusting these volunteers with a project whose successful completion is important to your organization. They will represent your organization to the public, and they will be entrusted with protecting your image as much as protecting your budget.

Resist the temptation to recruit from only one company or one group of friends. Consider a multitude of sources for your volunteers to avoid being dependent on one particular group or company. Change out volunteers from one project to another. If you have the same team with the same membership planning a special event or an appeal, over time you'll find staleness entering into the picture, with a potential negative impact to overall participation. While there's indeed a benefit to doing something consistently (donors know what to expect), you also need to recognize that changes in the economy and changes in society might be affecting your project or the way it's managed; then you need to react accordingly and make changes that will be beneficial to your organization. Sometimes a fresh set of eyes, or someone with a different background, can help you make those changes happen.

Plan for Turnover

The truth is, life will happen to your volunteers and some will not be able to stay with you for the full project. As you develop your team's charter and structure, include deputies to all key positions — these individuals should be ready to step in as needed. Invite them to committee meetings.

Sometimes you'll be put into the position where you need to invite a volunteer to depart from the project — sometimes for non-performance, other times to resolve conflicts. Again, you'll need to have a back-up plan that you can execute so that the project isn't harmed. When you must ask a volunteer to leave your project, you need to be tactful and sensitive to his or her privacy in sharing the departure news with the rest of your committee. It may be best to state that "so and so" is no longer able to participate and let it go at that.

Oversee Volunteer Performance

You expect volunteers to perform when they step forward and commit to complete a task that's important to achieving the project's goals. They likewise expect to be able to perform, to feel a sense of achievement, of meaningful contribution. This requires that both you and the volunteer understand what performance is expected of them. It's important that these expectations be documented in the volunteer position description and expressed in measurable terms. When recruiting a volunteer, provide the volunteer with the position description and give him or her time to review it; the volunteer must understand the performance expectations and be able and willing to meet them. You should then together review the position description to be sure that he or she understands and accepts the requirements.

You also need to consider how the volunteer's performance will be monitored so that you can address any issues quickly. Asking for periodic status reports, conducting one-on-one meetings — the same techniques used when monitoring employees — are appropriate. And if a volunteer is struggling with an assignment, is unable to provide the time required, or is missing some key skill, then consider how you might assist that volunteer — perhaps by asking another volunteer to work alongside them — before you decide that you need to replace the volunteer.

It's equally important for you to realize that these resources are volunteers, that this assignment is not their primary focus. There will be times when you'll need to be lenient and flexible. If a status report is missed, or if a sponsorship inquiry didn't happen as scheduled, but you know that these things will happen and the project's bigger target won't be affected, then remember that you're dealing with volunteers and let it go.

Deal with Non-Performing Volunteers

That said, you're responsible to the organization to ensure that the project is completed and that stakeholder objectives are met. This means that sometimes you'll just have to replace a disruptive or unsuitable volunteer. Do it the same way you would dismiss an employee — respect the individual, explain the reason for the dismissal, and offer another volunteer opportunity more aligned with his or her abilities or personality. As stated previously, when this situation occurs you need to be tactful and sensitive to the volunteer's privacy in sharing departure news with the rest of the committee.

Summary

Proper engagement with volunteers assigned to project work is critical to the success of the project. The organization is relying on the volunteers to assist staff in fulfilling the project's objectives, while relying on the project manager to ensure that the volunteers working on the project are properly engaged. The project manager needs to assume responsibility for that engagement and work with the volunteers so that the project is a positive experience not just for the organization but also for the volunteers. This is accomplished by ensuring that the right volunteer is assigned to the right activity at the right time, with the right amount of engagement and guidance from staff.

11

Recruiting and Retaining Reliable Volunteers

As stated in the previous chapter, recruiting and retaining good volunteers is critical to the overall success of many nonprofit organizations. Yet outside of some large health-care systems and national organizations, few nonprofits are able to establish a human resources department to oversee its volunteers and how they are recruited, assigned, and managed. Rather, these functions are left to the operational managers whose efforts require volunteer support.

Recruit the Best

When there is no volunteer department to assist with recruiting, superior project managers will select recruits from the volunteers with whom they have worked in the past. But if you're a new project manager you might not have a roster from which you can solicit resumes. One tool that you can easily adopt is to use a repository of the resumes of all past volunteers. If this repository is available electronically, you can search the resumes for key words culled from the position descriptions for the roles you're trying to fill. Ask people who are interested in volunteering for your organization to send you a "volunteer resume" that focuses on volunteer positions they have fulfilled in the past as well as their professional positions. Or have them complete a volunteer information form (see Figure 11.1).

Once you have information from your prospective volunteers you need to match your position description to their resumes or information forms and create a short-list of candidates with skills that align with your specific position needs. Approach those candidates with the volunteer opportunity, sharing the position description with them. Be sure they understand the commitment required of them, including the estimate of the time required to complete the necessary work and to attend meetings. If they're expected to purchase tickets to an event, or make a donation in support of a campaign, be sure that's also communicated. Not all potential committee volunteers will be in a position to "pay to play."

When recruiting volunteers, it's important to understand what a candidate brings to your organization. A review and discussion about their resume will permit you to understand their background and experiences. For instance, if they held a position in a retail environment, they might have excellent design skills and could be great on a decorations committee. Or if they held a finance position, perhaps they could handle the budget tracking and reporting for the project. You should also explore with the candidate what they enjoy doing. Maybe they want to do something that provides them with a chance to be creative or to apply some newly acquired skills. The important thing is to have the discussion and to understand the candidate's motivation and skill set.

Provide Leadership

If you're not the committee chair and project manager on the project, you need to pay particular attention to staffing the committee

VOLUNTEER INFORMATION FORM

Page 1 of 2

DATE: _____

NAME: _____
                       Last   First   Middle

ADDRESS: _____
                      Street   City   Zip Code

Home Phone #: _____ Emergency Contact: _____

Cell Phone #: _____ Name: _____

Business Phone #: _____ Phone #: _____

Company: _____ Relationship to you: _____

Job Title: _____

E-mail address: _____

Preferred Method of reaching you: ☐ Home Phone   ☐ Cell Phone   ☐ E-mail
(Please check one)

May we call you at work?   ☐ Yes   ☐ No

Skills — Please check all that apply:

☐ MS Office   ☐ Project management   ☐ Graphic design
☐ Journalism   ☐ Creative writing   ☐ Business writing
☐ Basic carpentry   ☐ Meeting planning   ☐ Telephone skills
☐ Able to drive   ☐ Finances/Budgets

Please list any others:

Please identify your availability for project team meetings; specify any time limitations (e.g., after 6:30 p.m., not Sundays):

Daytime: _____   Evenings: _____   Weekend: _____

All information contained on this form is confidential in nature and will not be shared except as needed in support of the volunteer assignment.

Figure 11.1. Volunteer information form, page one of two.

VOLUNTEER INFORMATION FORM

NAME: _____   DATE: _____

Please identify any past volunteer experiences you have had with us:

Have you volunteered for other organizations? If so, please identify and describe your responsibilities.

Why are you interested in volunteering with us? Please identify any skills you hope to develop in your time with us.

SIGNATURE: _____   DATE: _____

All information contained on this form is confidential in nature and will not be shared
except as needed in support of the volunteer assignment.

Figure 11.1. Volunteer information form, page two of two.

chair as well as the deputy chair. These volunteers need to have excellent people and communications skills. They should have demonstrated experience managing budgets as well as resolving conflicts. These individuals will be your project manager and deputy manager. Do interviews — multiple if needed — to ensure that you're assigning someone who will get the job done without alienating other volunteers or becoming the project's martyr. Recruit these positions first and then engage those volunteers in recruiting the other volunteers.

Mix It Up!

Consider a mixture of volunteers on your project team. Don't let the team become a clique of friends — you'll lose authority over your project. Also, a project team consisting of individuals with different backgrounds and experiences will bring variety to your project. The last thing you want a participant to say when receiving an appeal or event invitation is "Oh! I went to this last year, this looks like the same thing. I think I'll pass…." New volunteers supporting your project will bring new ideas so that each year's event is fresh and inviting to potential attendees.

Look for Future Board Members

As you work with your volunteers, consider how you might engage with them in the future. Some of your volunteers are looking for a meaningful relationship with your organization and the current assignment might just be the "let's see how this works" opportunity. Schedule discussions with the volunteers supporting your projects; understand their motivation and reasons for joining the project team. Consider how you might leverage their skills and knowledge on other projects — perhaps even on your board. You're making an investment in the volunteer; you'll want to retain that volunteer for future years.

Make the Volunteer Welcome

If the volunteer is new to your organization, schedule a tour with them. Provide literature and encourage them to explore the organization's website. You might consider inviting the new volunteer to meet others with whom they would interact, perhaps at an informal lunch or over coffee. If you already have a project team (committee) in place, the candidate should be invited to attend the next meeting to "try out" the committee before committing.

Don't dismiss volunteers after the project is concluded. Keep them connected to the organization between assignments. Invite them to attend information sessions to apprise them of your organization's activities such as staff changes, promotions, and overall organizational health. Actively seek their suggestions and inputs when planning.

Summary

Today people are overwhelmed with conflicting priorities and need to juggle their time. So it's important that nonprofit managers — both operations and project managers — artfully engage the volunteers they recruit. Volunteers are increasingly critical assets and, once obtained, should be nurtured and appropriately utilized. The volunteer who leaves an organization feeling unappreciated or misused is not only a lost volunteer but also potentially a lost donor and organization champion.

12

Five Rules of Effective Volunteer Engagement

Nonprofit organizations frequently find themselves relying on volunteers to work on projects necessary to obtain the funding required by the organization's mission. And in these days of decreased funding for staff positions, the use of volunteers is increasingly important.

Yet we tend to not practice good personnel management when interacting with volunteers. It's as if we place volunteers into a different resource class than our staff. Yes, volunteers are different — they don't collect a paycheck or certain other benefits from us. But they are indeed just as critical to our success. I've found that by applying the following five rules I've been able to obtain the best from every volunteer, and they've all had rewarding experiences.

RULE #1
Recruit the Right Volunteer for the Right Job

How many times have you expressed elation at filling a volunteer role only to later find yourself regretting it because the "found" body is not able to do the needed work? Filling a volunteer position on a project is just as crucial to a nonprofit's success as filling a paid position. Yet we're hesitant to apply the same level of discipline to the process of recruiting volunteers as we do in recruiting staff.

When recruiting to fill a volunteer position, we resist asking the candidate why they want the position. Instead we assume that they responded to our request because they share our passion about the organization's mission. The reality might be that they volunteered because they need to do community service or they want to be on a committee with one of their friends. Or they have some other reason. Without knowing the "why," it will be difficult for you to judge the individual's commitment or flexibility.

In addition to understanding the candidate's motivation for volunteering, you need to know what they can bring to your project. You need to have an open, one-on-one discussion with them about their background and experience so you'll know how they'll best fit your project management needs. Handle this discussion as you would an employment interview: schedule it in advance; conduct it in a professional environment; be prompt and courteous; do the appropriate follow-up. The following list identifies some of the questions I've found it useful to ask of the volunteer-candidate:

- How did you hear about our event? Our organization?
- Why do you want to volunteer here?
- Please describe your typical workday—what do you do?
- How available would you be in the evenings or weekends?
- Do you have access to a computer and a smartphone at home?
- What would make this volunteer activity a success for you?
- Please share your vision of the outcome (of the event, campaign, mailing, etc.)—what would success look like?
- Please tell me about your other volunteer activities?

One important note: If you're not the project manager but, instead, are recruiting the project manager (committee chairperson), recruit that position first and then be sure that the chairperson is involved in all subsequent recruiting activities. That chairperson is the individual who will be held responsible for the success or failure of your project so they need to be comfortable that the right folks are on their committee or project team.

RULE #2
Define the Job Clearly

Prepare a position description (see Figure 10.1 in Chapter 10) and review it with the volunteer. Be sure the description includes a clear discussion about expected performance, including security and confidentiality considerations as needed. If the volunteer is going to be using your organization's technology or facilities, be sure the position description explains their responsibilities regarding the safekeeping of that property. Ask the volunteer to read and observe any pertinent corporate policies, such as discrimination or harassment policies.

Once you've identified a qualified volunteer, be sure they know what's expected of them. Have a discussion about the anticipated effort, including frequency and location of mandatory meetings and other events. Share the project's work breakdown structure, if it exists, and other project documents, highlighting where the volunteer's efforts will fit in.

Finally, review the project's overall organizational structure with the volunteer. Give the volunteer a sense of what it will be like to work on the project. If you already have a project team in place, invite the candidate to attend the next meeting so that they can see if they really want to work with your team. You want to make sure that there will be no potential conflicts within the project team, that all assigned volunteers will be able to work together harmoniously.

There's always the risk of personality conflicts within project teams. Volunteer project teams, however, face additional potential conflicts. One such conflict might occur if you have representatives from competing businesses on your team. For instance, having representation from two restaurants might create friction when it comes to selecting an event caterer. Another source of conflict could arise if a similar project had been conducted in prior years and the former project manager or committee chair is on the current project team; they might tend to resist doing something different.

If you sense that there could be conflicts among your team members, perhaps one of the volunteers could be reassigned to another project supporting the organization, or maybe the potential conflict could be resolved by the project team members. For instance, if the conflict is related to business competition, one manner by which the conflict could be resolved would be for the parties to recuse themselves from discussions related to their businesses.

Just remember that, when building your project team, it's important to acknowledge that the risk of conflict exists and to ensure that it won't affect the project's performance.

RULE #3

Communicate Frequently (and Listen!)

Keeping volunteers informed and connected is the lifeline of your relationship. Communicate with them as frequently as you do your staff, and perhaps even more so! Remember, your staff members are connected to your organization's informal communications network, the volunteers are not. Let the volunteers know when there's a significant event within your organization, such as a reorganization or a promotion, even if it doesn't affect their project. It will make them feel that they're part of your organization and invested in its overall mission.

Schedule periodic one-on-one meetings with key volunteers and ask them how it's going. Be prepared to address their concerns and questions. During these meetings, I like to ask the volunteer if

---

FIVE RULES OF EFFECTIVE VOLUNTEER ENGAGEMENT

RULE #1   Recruit the Right Volunteer for the Right Job

RULE #2   Define the Job Clearly

RULE #3   Communicate Frequently (and Listen!)

RULE #4   Be Prepared to Reassign a Volunteer

RULE #5   Cultivate Good Volunteers

Figure 12.1. Follow these five rules of good personnel management to obtain the best from every volunteer.

they understand how important their contribution is to the team and to the organization, whether they've met the project's sponsor, are they acquiring any new skills, and are they feeling happy about the work they're doing. Use this meeting to determine if this person is a volunteer you can, and want to, approach for the next project.

Reinforce communications within the project teams. Consider leveraging technology such as Facebook or Twitter to support communications among team members. They can use it to keep each other apprised of progress. If you're the project manager, conduct team meetings on a regular schedule, at a time and location that's convenient for the majority of the team. Distribute meeting agendas and handouts at least 24 hours before the meeting so that attendees can be prepared. Distribute meeting minutes within 24 hours after the meeting.

RULE #4
Be Prepared to Reassign a Volunteer

Unfortunately, we occasionally need to change our volunteer assignments. Perhaps the volunteer isn't able to perform as needed or there's a conflict of personalities, or there's a greater need for help on another aspect of the project. When this occurs discuss the issue with the volunteer. Remember, this is someone who has shown sufficient interest in your mission to join the project team, to invest their time and effort. You owe it to this person to explain honestly why the change is needed. Together you should explore ways that the volunteer can continue to support the project if that's what the volunteer wants. If there's truly no suitable role for the volunteer on that particular project, you should explore other projects within your organization that might be better suited to the volunteer's abilities.

If the change is needed because team dynamics are not working in the best interest of your mission, you should determine whether the volunteer is suited to your organization at all. If he or she is, then do your best to identify another position that would work for them. If you think the volunteer is not appropriate for your organization, then you need to gracefully thank them for their efforts and explain that there's a mismatch between their work approach and the culture of your organization.

Dismissing someone can be a difficult task — it's never easy or pleasant, but you must do it for the sake of your mission. If you feel uncomfortable holding these discussions, or if you're not sure what to say to the volunteer, ask someone in your personnel department or management team to provide you with coaching and to let you do some role-playing as you prepare to take action.

RULE #5

Cultivate Good Volunteers

It might be trite but it's worth saying: A volunteer in the hand is worth two in the bush. Good volunteers are a scarce commodity. You need to invest in your volunteers, cultivate them, groom them, and grow them. Give some thought as to how you're going to keep a good volunteer who's interested and connected with your organization upon completion of the current project assignment. Is there another role they can perform for you? Are they a candidate for a more influential role, such as serving on an advisory group or a board? Can they take on increasing responsibility and manage a project for you? Develop a volunteer progression plan for them, increasing their role within your organization.

Be certain to thank ALL volunteers, frequently and sincerely — especially those who are good performers — and let them know that they're truly appreciated. Recognize them as contributors to your organization's goals. These volunteers are not giving money, but they're giving their time, an equally important resource for your organization.

Case Study: The Volunteer-Managed Project

I had been asked to serve as a volunteer project manager for a two-year volunteer effort culminating in the successful production of an international conference. This activity was conducted during the time period in which the organization was growing in membership and in event participation, transitioning from a small, volunteer-managed association to an international association and addressing the challenges resulting from that transition. Some key attributes of the program included the following:

- It was a nonprofit function.
- It was run by volunteers with managerial/executive day jobs.
- It was important to retain volunteer engagement over an extended period of time.
- It was particularly challenging to schedule and keep the project on track given the volunteer workforce's day-job commitments.

Recognizing the importance of this volunteer undertaking and realizing that my job would require travel during the planning period, I asked the association's leadership to identify a co-project manager, someone who could ensure the project's continued progress in my absence and someone with experience with conference planning. In hindsight, this was one of the best risk mitigation actions taken. Having two managers provided team members with continuous leadership and timely decision making. A key factor in the success of this management approach was an agreement between my co-manager and me to not let our egos enter into the relationship and to support each other's decisions once a decision was made.

The project's core team consisted of sixteen volunteers, supplemented by the association's full-time meeting planner and a team from the association's publishing department responsible for publishing the conference proceedings. The volunteers, who in their day jobs were all senior managers with full-time jobs, most of which required travel, brought with them enormous skill sets and enormous challenges. These volunteers were solicited from members of the association's local chapters and from personal contacts within the association. Early team-building sessions and an *ego box* where egos were checked at the door were essential in bringing this virtual team together to develop a vision and theme. It was a volunteer team structure that was adopted by subsequent symposia teams.

☑ QUICK TIP

An *ego box* is a cardboard box, covered in tinfoil, with a slot in the top and a sign hanging over it that says "Place egos here!" The box sits outside the project team meeting room. It serves as a visual reminder that team members are peers without titles once entering that room.

We had a volunteer dedicated to overseeing the project's financial status who worked with the association's financial office. Unlike other volunteer projects with which I had been involved, this one required the local project team to maintain a checking account and to receive and dispense funds from that account as needed. The volunteer we selected to perform this task for us was in a trusted position in his employment so we were comfortable with him in this role. Otherwise I would have asked for a police background check to ensure fiduciary reliability. The monthly bank statements were provided by the volunteer to my co-manager and me, with a copy of the project's budget reports and financial statements on a quarterly basis.

Our project charter was provided by the association's board of directors. Not only did it contain the fixed dates and location of the conference, it also included anticipated profit targets for the event. This conference was the association's largest revenue generator. As with any event project, it had multiple drop-dead schedule constraints, not just

 **GLOSSARY**

Timeboxed schedules are schedules for projects designed to fit within specific timeframes. The project's scope is defined by answering questions such as: "What can we accomplish in the next three months?"

for the event itself but for contracting outside services, production and distribution of marketing and registration materials, and the publication of the conference proceedings.

With these pre-determined deadlines and volunteer team members, risk planning and communications planning were essential to identify, gather, and mitigate potential issues. These are often dispensed with in volunteer projects and yet they are probably more critical in this situation. With volunteer-managed projects, unlike employee-managed projects, natural communications channels are not developed and escalation and risk mitigation paths are non-existent. In this project, in order to assure timely execution, the core project management team established status report templates, used technology to optimize disparate schedules, *timeboxed schedules,* and developed inputs and outputs for all meetings to keep things productive (the regular meetings focused on raising issues that could impact execution and on resolving issues that stood in the way of success).

Each core team member was asked to form a sub-team to support their area of the project and to hold separate team meetings to focus on their particular tasks. This allowed the core project management team to focus on the big-picture decisions that needed to be made. It also provided each core team member with an opportunity to identify a deputy to attend core team meetings in lieu of, or in addition to, the core team member. The availability of this deputy was particularly useful when summer vacations and business travel occurred.

Each sub-team was provided with a charter clarifying their decision-making authorities, their budget, and their expected deliverables. This use of sub-teams became particularly important when it was time to review abstracts from candidate speakers for the actual conference. With over 500 technical paper submissions to be reviewed by subject-matter experts within a thirty-day window, these additional volunteers were engaged by the core team member (whose role was technical program manager), who made assignments, followed up on them, and kept that team focused on their tasks. This intense oversight by the technical program manager permitted the rest of us to stay focused on our individual assignments and not get into the details of reviewing abstracts. The technical program manager also worked with his sub-team to manage all the logistics associated with the technical program, which included scheduling speakers and equipment and coordinating with the publications team to ensure that the final papers were received on time and in the format needed for publication.

As mentioned above, the association sponsoring the project was undergoing substantial growth, leading to management and cultural changes. All of this flux was an added challenge to executing the project. Maintaining communications with stakeholders and formalizing how problems would be solved were important elements in keeping the project rolling and on track. My co-manager and I worked out a schedule of report updates and broader communications such as newsletters and project highlights, which alternated on a monthly basis, to keep all stakeholders apprised of the project's progress and the key decisions that the core project management team had made. These reports also included budget reports.

The results were outstanding. As optimistic as the team was, they beat even their own expectations.

- The conference experienced the highest attendance to date, far exceeding profit expectations.

- The team structure and processes were able to deliver a larger, more professional conference. These practices were used for the next ten years, and the technical program management handbook and volunteer structure are still used today.

- During the two-year project the volunteer project team needed no replacements, didn't suffer from the usual burnout, and went on to be very active in the local and regional association components.

Summary

Volunteers are critical to your project success. You need to ensure that you treat them well. By following the five rules discussed above you will maximize the value your volunteers provide and the benefits they receive by working with you.

PART FOUR

Governance in Your Project-Based Nonprofit

13

Project Management Office Functions

Now that we've discussed what project management is, how to apply it to your organization's efforts, and how to manage your project volunteers, it's time to talk about the role that the leadership of your organization plays in ensuring the successful management of its projects.

The Project Management Office

Many organizations, especially larger ones, have found the establishment of a formal project management office (PMO) to be of value. Research has shown that organizations with PMOs report significantly more projects coming in on time and on budget and meeting intended goals, improvements in productivity, and increased cost savings compared to those without a PMO (PM Solutions Research, 2012; Project Management Institute, 2011; Forrester Research, 2011; ESI International, 2011).

Just as there are different forms of organizations, there are several forms of PMOs. The PMO can be part of the organization's strategy-setting team, identifying projects aligned with the organization's strategies. The PMO can be a support function, supporting project managers with processes, tools, and training. The PMO can also be a line unit, providing project managers for specific projects. Or it can be a business unit that provides all of the above.

In his PMI award-winning book, *The Strategic Project Office: A Guide to Improving Organizational Performance,* Kent Crawford identifies six primary PMO functions: processes/standards/methodologies, project management software tools, project managers, consulting/mentoring, project support, and training (see Figure 13.1). It's important to note that for project management to be successful you need to address each of these functions to some degree, whether you have a PMO or not, and even if you're an agile nonprofit. The maintenance of repeatable practices and effective tools and support, as well as the leadership of experienced managers, all contribute to the success of your organization's projects.

The PMO in Your Agile Nonprofit

Your agile nonprofit needs to consider the risks it faces with its projects and identify the PMO functions most critical to success. In most nonprofits those functions will include the establishment of basic common practices, standardized project and portfolio reporting, integrated volunteer engagement and oversight, and mentoring and training. And while it might be nice to have a centralized PMO to oversee these functions, the reality is that many nonprofits cannot carry the associated overhead. Rather, these functions will be integrated into the job responsibilities of existing staff, primarily the chief development officer or operations manager, plus the human resource manager and the volunteer manager (if there is one).

In addition to implementing the practices described in Part Two of this book, you'll want to establish just enough project management practices to minimize the overhead of reporting project status and maintaining the project portfolio. Some best practices to be considered include:

PROJECT MANAGEMENT OFFICE FUNCTIONS	
Function	**Description**
Processes/ Standards/ Methodologies	Project management methodology maintenance and support, standard reporting and controls, lessons learned, project governance/portfolio management, project management "community of practice"
Project Management Software Tools	Deployment of enterprise project tracking tools, templates and repositories, help desk, establishment of common "project language" (i.e., common chart of accounts, common coding conventions)
Project Managers	Supplemental expert project managers
Consulting/ Mentoring	Assistance with methodology application, knowledge sharing, assistance to "troubled projects," project assessments and audits
Project Support	Project controls expertise, project initiation/planning expertise, project tracking and reporting, project management tools assistance
Training	Project management training, methodology training, establishing a career development program

Figure 13.1. Project management office functions.

- All status reports are placed in a central repository on the same day in the same format.
- All status reports are easily accessed by any project stakeholder.
- A project portfolio calendar/spreadsheet is updated at the same time each month.

By establishing consistent reporting in a manner that provides consistent information to all stakeholders you will minimize the thrashing around that frequently occurs as stakeholders query different sources for project information. Adapting the use of a portfolio wall is one such easy solution, as long as the information currency is maintained.

The Portfolio Wall

A portfolio wall is a centralized location within the work area where current project status information for all active projects is portrayed. In addition, all future projects are identified with a description of their objectives, their anticipated start date, and the name of their sponsor or owner. The use of a portfolio wall enables project team members to not only review the current status of their own project but also understand where it fits into the organization's overall priorities. It also enables project managers — be they volunteers or staff members — to know what other projects are underway, thereby enabling collaboration and communication across projects. For instance, one project manager might notice another project's next major activity is a mailing at the same time as his or her project's mailing. Combining the mailings might be a means of saving costs.

Integrated Volunteer Engagement

Many nonprofits have a manager responsible for all volunteer engagement. If there's no such position in your organization, then the specific responsibilities associated with that role should be assigned to a member of the operations management staff so that your organization stays engaged with volunteers between assignments. The volunteer manager should work with the organization's managers to establish a uniform volunteer recognition program and to ensure that your organization's volunteer policies are in alignment with local and federal labor laws. This manager assists with the recruiting of your volunteers and works with your project managers on volunteer assignments based on the volunteers' skills and interests.

Training and Mentoring

An important function typically associated with a PMO is the development of leadership and project management skills within the organization. Within the nonprofit organization this means providing training and mentoring not only to staff members but also to volunteers performing the role of project manager. Formal classroom training, on-site workshops, and professional association memberships are ways in which technical project management training can be obtained.

People frequently learn new skills and adopt new practices, however, only to lapse into old behaviors and approaches when the application of the new is "too hard" or when time pressures are introduced. It's during those times that an active mentor can reinforce the new, encouraging their protégé to continue to apply the new skills and practices. A mentor is defined as someone who is "a wise or trusted counselor or teacher." Project management mentors provide support by imparting to their protégés the wisdom they've gained through experience and continued learning. Your organization, therefore, should establish a formal mentoring program for its project managers, to reinforce classroom training and to aid in their further development, either to become more senior staff members or, in the case of volunteers, potential board members.

Summary

For-profit organizations have recognized the benefit of the functions typically found within a project management office and have made PMOs a core management structure in their organizations. While it's not necessary for your nonprofit to establish a formal PMO, the performance of the key functions of that office, especially those related to the oversight and development of project management capabilities, will enhance the overall performance of your organization.

14

Leveraging Your Project Portfolio

C an nonprofits continue to operate the same way they've operated in the past, given the ever-increasing demands being placed on them? Should they take a more business-like approach? In other words, should effective portfolio management be a best practice for nonprofit organizations? If so, then what are the changes needed in nonprofit organizational behavior — at the organization level, the director level, the management level, and the volunteer level? What education is required? How is this facilitated?

In previous chapters I stated that leaders of nonprofit organizations find themselves being asked to do more with less and to be agile in making decisions. Applying the discipline of project portfolio management enables the chief development officer to be responsive to these demands in a calm and effective manner. The project portfolio will advise the chief development officer which staff members or volunteers are working on what, which ones are available for assignment, and what other projects would be impacted should a staff member or volunteer be assigned to a project or re-assigned to a different project. A well-maintained project portfolio will enable your organization to be positioned to deal with the unexpected.

Similar to a financial portfolio, a project portfolio is a list of the investments your organization is making in project-based work. A fully-functional portfolio communicates the priorities, returns on investment, and budgets for the projects your organization is undertaking to achieve its strategic and operational objectives.

Project portfolio management (PPM) is defined as the continuous process of identifying, selecting, and managing a portfolio of projects in alignment with key performance metrics and strategic business objectives. It's about "doing the right things right."

Project Portfolio Management and Strategic Planning

Effectively managing your project portfolio requires clear, consistent, and constant communications as well as complete integration of all the organization's business plans and budgets. When developing your nonprofit's strategic plan, your executive team needs to consider what it takes to actually run the organization — that is, what it takes to perform the day-to-day operations associated with your organization's mission. Each manager should be asked to determine the tasks performed by each position and to rank those tasks relative to their contribution to the overall mission. Tasks that have little impact on the mission should be challenged; perhaps those are tasks that should no longer be performed by staff; perhaps they should be performed by volunteers or not performed at all.

Upon completion of this analysis, the executive team, the managers, and the board will understand what resources are required to sustain the organization. This requirement should be reflected in the organization's overall plans and those resources blocked off (considered unavailable for use) when planning your strategies. The remaining resources can then be allocated to strategic initiatives — to be managed through the application of project management practices.

One challenge faced by nonprofit organizations is staying focused. Volunteers, donors, and other stakeholders will come forward with suggestions for projects, some aligned with the organization's mission, some not aligned. It's imperative that your board and chief development officer acquire the skills needed to assess and address these suggestions. They need to have the ability to keep an open mind when being pitched an idea, to understand if there's merit in the idea, and the ability to gently let the idea-owner know if the idea doesn't align with current plans. Sometimes, however, a suggested project is one that merits placement into the organization's portfolio. That means that the suggested project is more strategic than another project in the portfolio, and that other project is then not undertaken. The ability to inform the project sponsor and stakeholders of its suspension, or to tell a donor that their project is not aligned with the organization's strategy, requires great communication skills. You want to be able to explain, potentially in detail, why the project is not going to proceed. This means being able to express the decision in terms of the organization's current strategic objectives or current resources and capabilities, without attacking the project itself or giving false expectations that it might be entertained in the future.

Your Portfolio and Staff

Each year, as part of your organization's budget cycle, your executive team reviews and updates your organization's strategic objectives for the upcoming year. They also determine how much funding should be available for day-to-day operations. These decisions determine how staff time should be allocated.

When translating the strategic objectives into a cohesive fundraising program, for example, a manager should consider these allocations. Suppose your executive team has determined that acquiring new cardiac equipment is the number one objective for your healthcare system; then your development office should ensure that the fundraising projects (appeals, special events, etc.) in support of this endeavor are adequately staffed and resourced. Throughout the year, as work assignments are reviewed and made, it should be kept in mind which staff are be available to work on which projects. A documented project portfolio enables the manager to do this. Your project portfolio clearly identifies each activity associated with the cardiac equipment acquisition and the people assigned to work on those activities. This visibility allows the manager to know that those people are working on the organization's most strategic objective.

How Do You Do It?

Managing using a project portfolio consists of three phases — initiate/plan, execute, and control — as shown in Figure 14.1.

The initiate/plan phase begins with an affirmation by your organization's leadership that a project portfolio would be of benefit to your organization and that you will adopt the use of it into your decision process. Once that decision is made, your leadership needs to define the content of the project portfolio. It might be that not all projects are of a magnitude or impact that they need to be tracked as separate activities — perhaps they should be grouped into one entry in the portfolio. An example of this class of project is a quarterly CEO presentation to the business community. While it's a project and should be planned as one, it might involve only the CEO, his or her administrative assistant, and someone from your public relations department — not a tremendous use of resources and not something that the leadership team needs to monitor the performance of. On the other hand, an annual holiday gift drive is very visible to the community, consumes many volunteer and staff hours, and is something your leadership team should be on top of.

After defining the types, or classes, of projects to be monitored, your leadership team needs to establish the criteria by which they'll monitor the performance of those projects: budget,

PROJECT PORTFOLIO MANAGEMENT PHASES

Initiate/Plan Phase
- Confirm commitment
- Define the portfolio
- Develop criteria/measures
- Prepare the environment

Execute Phase
- Identify current projects
- Prioritize projects
- Approve or cancel current projects
- Add new projects

Control Phase
- Track performance of portfolio projects
- Make corrective actions as needed

Figure 14.1. Project portfolio management phases.

resource consumption, schedule, etc. For instance, do they want to be notified when a project is more than ten percent over budget? Or when a project is more than five days late in meeting a milestone? And if they're notified, are they prepared to assist in resolving whatever issues the project team is confronting? The criteria you select should align with your organization's overall performance measurement, so that you can determine the impact the project's performance is having on the organization. I recommend the criteria be kept to no more than three, so that reporting can remain agile. Budget performance, schedule performance, and the top three most-likely risks are the ones I like to monitor when given the choice.

These criteria and the support that's available need to be shared with all staff and volunteer project managers so that they appreciate the importance of controlling their assigned projects and of effectively communicating the status of those activities to your organization's leadership.

Establish Your Project Portfolio

The development of a portfolio is straightforward for most organizations. I encourage my clients to adopt the "keep it simple" mindset. Although there are some very sophisticated project portfolio management technology tools available, I find they're overly complicated for most nonprofits. A simple spreadsheet posted to a common bulletin board for all to see is frequently all that's needed to show the progress of your portfolio (see Figure 14.2).

When establishing the portfolio you should first identify the work that must be done, such as regulatory projects, and make them the first priority for resource allocation. Then survey your staff; ask them what they're working on, for whom, and when it's expected to be completed. Find the hidden projects that every organization has, the work that came in via a request in the hallway or in a casual conversation with a donor. Then determine the nature of the project — is there an active sponsor? Does the project have funding available to see it through to completion? Does it align with the organization's strategic objectives? If the answer to any of these questions is "no," then it would probably be wise to cancel the effort and inform the requestor why.

As you survey the work underway try to understand the nature of the people working on the project. If the project is heavily volunteer-staffed with no paid staff hours supporting it, then perhaps you can authorize it to continue as an external, volunteer-based

GLOSSARY

Mandated projects are projects that must be performed to remain in compliance with laws, regulations, and other statutory requirements. One such project could be updating the language in all solicitations to clarify IRS guidance.

Strategic projects are projects that further the mission and the strategic objectives of the nonprofit, such as a walk-a-thon to support a capital campaign.

Operational projects are projects that enhance the operations of the nonprofit. A typical operational project could be the update of the office's technology.

PROJECT PORTFOLIO MANAGEMENT REPORT

Priority	Project	Status	Sponsor	Project Manager	Benefit	Cost Estimate	% Complete	Status Summary
3	Blackbaud Migration (Reporting Phase)	Okay	J. Smith	C. Johnson	Improve efficiencies	$500,000	99%	Cleaning up data & loose ends
4	Wine Tasting Event (February 2012)	Okay	S. Long	B. Marks	Cardiology Unit	$45,000	74%	Soliciting sponsors
1	Christmas Appeal Mailing	Resource Challenged	M. Jones	B. Marks	Pediatrics	$50,000	50%	Resource conflicts, behind schedule
2	Holiday Gala (12/1/11)	Resource Challenged	M. Jones	B. Marks	Pediatrics	$250,000	50%	Need more sponsors & board engagement
5	Annual Report (January 2012)	Okay	J. Smith	C. Johnson	Donor stewardship	$100,000	10%	Beginning design
8	Office Renovations	On Hold	V. Lasalle	TBD	Maintenance	$500,000	Delayed by COO until after holidays	
6	Disaster Recovery/ Business Continuity	On Hold	J. Smith	TBD	Risk avoidance	$85,000	Pending budget for consultant & completion of Blackbaud	
7	Spring Appeal	Pending	S. Long	TBD	TBD	unknown	Will start planning upon completion of Holiday Gala	

Figure 14.2. Project portfolio management report. The report gives you quick insight into the status of your major projects. In this report you can see that the number one priority project is behind schedule because of resource challenges.

project and ask the volunteer leader to keep you informed. If the effort is consuming staff time then it needs to be sanctioned within your portfolio since it's consuming a portion of your budget.

A well-balanced portfolio will consist of a mix of *mandated projects, strategic projects* and *operational projects* — both current and future projects. And appropriate budget dollars will have been allocated to cover the resources required to execute and deliver on the portfolio.

Manage with Your Project Portfolio

A project portfolio is akin to your financial portfolio and requires the same level of management discipline if good results are to be achieved. A generally accepted practice is to update your project portfolio with the latest project status information monthly, taking corrective action as needed. Use the information in the portfolio report to inform your decisions: Do we have the resources to undertake another program? Is there capacity for another special event? What would we trade to make those resources available?

Don't hesitate to make hard decisions about projects using your portfolio. Be sure your resources are allocated to strategic projects, not pet projects. There can only be one Priority #1 project. If a project is no longer aligned with objectives, or demonstrates that it won't be able to achieve its objectives, don't hesitate to cancel it. A project cancelled in a timely manner can be as effective as a completed one if the cancellation releases resources for a higher-priority project.

Use project priorities to help you make decisions about resource assignments. Two golden rules I recommend applying are: don't have individuals work on more than two or three projects concurrently; and avoid "thrashing" — that is, don't start/stop/start projects to make key resources available. To free up key resources focus instead on achieving a project's objectives as quickly as possible. Use volunteers and board members appropriately. Leverage board members and their relationships on strategic efforts; use staff members on mandated projects. Watch out for volunteer-managed projects that migrate into staff-managed projects. Question the business case for each project, especially volunteer projects. Cancel volunteer projects (diplomatically!) if they consume an inordinate amount of staff time or create resource conflicts with strategic or mandated projects.

Share Information on Your Project Portfolio

It's important to share information on the approved project portfolio with your staff, your volunteers, and your stakeholders. They all like to know what's being worked on, what the priorities for the organization are, how their efforts fit into that bigger picture, and how they might help out.

When communicating the status of your organization's portfolio, not only should each project's name and schedule be disclosed, but also each project's priority, its sponsors and project managers, the benefits to be expected, and its current status (you can use color in addition to words to show status — green to signify everything's okay, yellow to signify there are problems, and red to show that the project is on hold).

In Figure 14.2 you can see that the number one priority project is behind schedule because of resource conflicts. The sponsor of the project, Dr. Jones, has been trying to obtain wording from the designated patient family for the appeal, but that individual has just not been responsive. When the chief development officer learns of this, she can volunteer to assist in obtaining the wording or suggest an alternative source for the appeal wording.

Case Study: Project Portfolio Management

In the foundation's start-up years, many volunteer-managed activities had been undertaken, sometimes with board knowledge, sometimes without, leading to varying degrees of success. One activity resulted in the creation of marketing materials that the foundation was unable to use because the messaging wasn't aligned with the foundation's mission. Another activity, while well-intended, resulted in a tremendous administrative burden for the foundation's support staff and wasn't sustainable within the foundation's operating budget. And in yet another situation, a project upon which the foundation was relying went awry, and its final objectives were never achieved, partially due to the lack of staff oversight of the volunteers.

After some years of maturing, the foundation's board found itself in the position of being able to refine the foundation's overall mission and to establish specific focus areas for its work. Each of these focus areas was supported by donors and other stakeholders from around the globe. This broad reach of support resulted in many suggestions for specific projects in support of each area. However, the foundation had limited staff capacity to oversee projects, even those that were volunteer-managed activities.

The board decided to apply the principles of project portfolio management to address the lessons learned from those early efforts. Applying project portfolio management would provide a means by which the board could determine which of the suggested projects the foundation would undertake in the current year, which ones would be deferred, and which could be transferred to other entities for execution. The board began the process by collecting all project ideas that had been submitted to the foundation's office or to individual directors. These ideas, plus ideas the directors had also developed, were then aligned with each of the program areas. If the project didn't support one of the areas, it was considered a potential for the future and automatically deferred to future years. Then the board went through a series of prioritization exercises, where each suggested project's priority was considered within its program area. The top three projects in each area were then compared against each other to create a list that represented the combined priorities. Funding was then allocated from the top down, until the budget that had been established for project activities was consumed. Those projects that were in the top nine, but below the funding line, were retained within the portfolio in the event funding became available. The other prioritized projects within each program area were also kept in the portfolio, but in a deferred status.

Applying the project portfolio management practices of prioritization and oversight provided the foundation:

- The discipline required to ensure that projects were aligned with the organization's overall mission and strategies

- Knowledge of the organization's priorities and which projects were approved in support of those priorities

- A framework by which decisions on how to use the foundation's donations could be made

Summary

Project portfolio management is indeed a best practice performed by many for-profit industry leaders. It encourages an organization to allocate its resources, and thereby the work, to those activities and projects that contribute most significantly to the achievement of the organization's strategic objectives.

The lack of a project portfolio management approach can result in an organization that's chaotic, misses opportunities, burns through resources, and doesn't achieve its strategic goals (see Figure 14.3).

THE RISK OF HAVING NO PROJECT PORTFOLIO MANAGEMENT

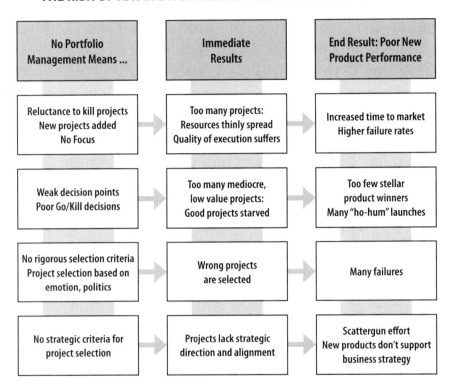

Figure 14.3. A lack of project portfolio management leads to poor performance in new products or services.

15

The Role of Your Board and Other Project Sponsors

It's characteristic of nonprofit organizations to operate under the oversight of a board of directors. These individuals are often asked to serve on the board because of their passion and willingness to support the mission of the organization. Typically they're executives or community leaders with experience in setting strategic direction and aligning operational plans to that direction.

However, in the project-based nonprofit organization, the directors have the following additional responsibilities to fulfill:

- Create and communicate the organization's plans for the year, including any strategic objectives.
- Select and sponsor projects to implement strategy.
  - Approve business cases.
  - Approve project charters.
  - Review high-impact projects.
- Prioritize projects on a continuing basis.
- Communicate changes in strategy and priorities to project managers.
- Co-own projects and participate in their oversight.

Project Sponsor Responsibilities

The Project Management Institute (2013) defines a project sponsor as "the person or group who provides resource and support for the project and is accountable for enabling success…. From initial conception through project closure, the sponsor promotes the project."

A significant responsibility of the project sponsor is to allocate the financial resources required by the project team. In many organizations this means that the project sponsor is responsible for developing the financial justification for the project, with inputs from the project manager as to the estimated project costs based on the scope defined by the sponsor. If the available funds are not sufficient to meet the project costs, then the sponsor needs to redefine the project scope, working with the project manager and the team until the scope fits the available funds.

Usually the project sponsor acts on behalf of the organization to approve the project charter, authorizing the project manager to begin spending funds on the project. However, in some organizations this authorization might be delegated to the operations manager or someone in charge of the philanthropy office's activities. It's important to note that while the authority to sign might be delegated, the actual authorization still must come from the project sponsor.

Another significant role the project sponsor needs to fulfill is that of the project champion. The sponsor needs to assist the project manager in identifying opportunities to improve project performance as well as potential risks that might curtail overall performance and ways to mitigate those risks. The former frequently entails highlighting other projects underway that might contribute to a project's success, such as leveraging another project's marketing collateral and thereby saving on costs. The latter might mean assisting the project team in identifying additional resources that might be needed to complete the project. Being able to provide this level of active sponsorship to the project requires that the project sponsor possess an active understanding of the project's current status, risks, and issues, an understanding best obtained by participating in the project team's status meetings and having regular communications with the project manager.

One challenge that many project teams encounter is the unavailability of the project sponsor when a key decision needs to be made. Should a project sponsor not be available, the project manager needs to be able to obtain that decision from an authorized delegate or be empowered to make the decision himself or herself. The project manager, in order to be able to comfortably make that decision, needs to feel that he or she understands the organization's strategic objectives and how this project fits into the picture. Hence the project sponsor needs to be able to share that information with the project team as a whole and especially with the project manager. Likewise, the sponsor needs to communicate organizational changes. I recall one project on which I worked that was going to be significantly impacted by an organizational realignment. The project sponsor was aware of the pending realignment but wasn't in a position to share it with our team. As a result, some decisions our team made resulted in wasted volunteer efforts and disgruntled volunteers.

Project Governance Responsibilities

Project governance is defined as those activities needed to establish strategies, performance objectives, and the alignment of projects with those strategies. Depending on the maturity of your nonprofit, your board might find itself in the position of providing governance to the projects underway. In other cases your senior management might provide project governance. Provision of project governance means that your board or senior management actively reviews status information, budgets, and certain deliverables, to ensure alignment with the project's initial charter and the nonprofit's objectives (see Figure 15.1).

149

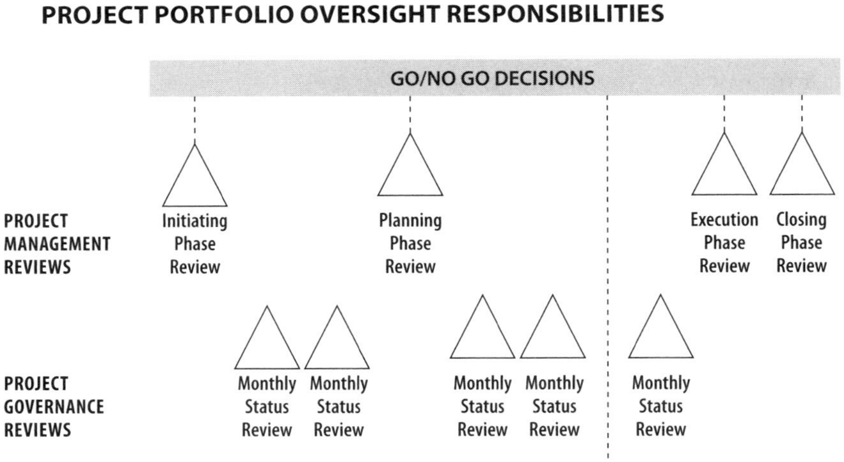

PROJECT PORTFOLIO OVERSIGHT RESPONSIBILITIES

Figure 15.1. Project management reviews, conducted by the project manager's management, are focused on the application of project management practices, especially the thoroughness of project plans and controls. Project governance reviews, typically conducted by the project sponsor, are focused on the project's overall performance towards its stated objectives.

Portfolio Oversight Responsibilities

In addition to sponsoring projects, your board members should provide oversight and guidance relative to your project portfolio. They should be prepared to receive and review project status information, to make the hard decisions and not approve projects that aren't aligned with your organization's strategic objectives or necessary for continued operations.

Saying "no" in a politic manner to a donor who wants to provide money to the organization for a project that's not aligned with the overall mission should be the responsibility of a member of your board, not a member of your staff. And when approving projects, your board should ensure that donor stewardship is considered, that funds being applied to an initiative are available to use on that project.

Summary

A nonprofit's board or senior management team plays an integral role in the overall success of the organization's projects by ensuring that the right projects are chartered, that changes in the organization's strategies are communicated in a timely manner, and that guidance is provided to project teams when requested. Active participation in the review of the organization's portfolio and the appropriate provision of resources are key functions of the role.

GOING FORWARD

In the introduction to this book, my associate Pamela Puleo presented several reasons why nonprofit organizations that desire to be agile in today's hectic world should learn and apply the basic concepts of project management. She addressed the challenges of doing more with less — less funding available for operations, less staff time available to undertake extra work. She also reminded us of the reality that volunteers are rare commodities today.

As managers, you are obligated to do your utmost to be careful stewards of the organizational resources provided to you in support of your projects. Those resources, be they staff hours, volunteer hours, or actual dollars, could have been applied directly to the organization's mission. Instead they were given to you, to use those resources to generate a return to the organization. It is your responsibility to ensure that those resources are used for maximum benefit to your organization, and that the staff and volunteers have a positive experience in their assignments and remain loyal to and supportive of the organization. It is your responsibility to achieve the project outcomes to which you agreed. The practice of certain project management and volunteer management techniques as described in the preceding chapters will enable you to fulfill these responsibilities.

So explore the ideas and practices I've shared with you in this book. Try them out. Adapt them to fit the needs of your projects and your organization. We're each unique, with unique approaches to completing our tasks, and what works for me might not work for you. What will work for you, however, are the processes associated with initiating, planning, executing, monitoring and controlling, and then formally closing your projects. Just as good chefs adapt recipes and make them their own, you should do the same with the tools I've presented here — adapt them to support your adoption of the project management processes and approaches described in this book.

These processes and approaches have been applied successfully in many industries, in for-profit and government organizations. Now it's time for your nonprofit organization to adopt them.

REFERENCES

Center for Business Practices (2006). *The State of Project Management 2006: A Benchmark of Current Business Practices.* Glen Mills, PA: Center for Business Practices.

Crawford, J. K. (2010). *Strategic Project Office: A Guide to Improving Organizational Performance, Second Edition.* Boca Raton, FL: CRC Press.

ESI International (2011). *The Global State of the PMO: Its Value, Effectiveness and Role as the Hub of Training.* Arlington, VA: ESI International.

Forrester Research (2011). *The State of the PMO in 2011.* Cambridge, MA: Forrester Research.

McLean, C. & Brouwer, C. (2012). *The Effect of the Economy On the Nonprofit Sector.* Williamsburg, VA: GuideStar.

PM Solutions Research (2012). *The State of the PMO 2012.* Glen Mills, PA: PM Solutions.

Project Management Institute (2011). *Pulse of the Profession.* Newtown Square, PA: Project Management Institute.

Project Management Institute (2013). *A Guide to the Project Management Body of Knowledge (PMBOK®), 5th Edition.* Newtown Square, PA: Project Management Institute.

Urban Institute (2012). *The Nonprofit Sector in Brief: Public Charities, Giving, and Volunteering.* Washington, DC: Urban Institute.

INDEX

resources
  agile management of, 22–23
  definition, 22–23
results-focused, importance of, 87
risk
  identification and analysis, 65–66
  in project, 64–70
  responses to, 64–65
risk log, 66
risk mitigation, 66
  in project life cycle model, 38, 41
risk planning, 123–124
risk response log
  example, 67f
  instructions, 68f
risk response log, detailed
  example, 69f
  instructions, 70f
schedule
  developing, 52–54
  milestones, 53
  must meet dates, 53
scope
  definition, 28
  how to define, 31–33
skills development, and the project
  management office, 133
SMART, and setting objectives, 31f
social media
  and nonprofits, 91–92
  tactics, 93f–95f
social roles, changes in, 7–9
special event project publicity, 48
staff, responsibilities of, 24–26
status report
  example, 43f
  what to include, 42

strategic differentiators, definition, 76
strategic objectives, 137–138
strategic projects, definition, 140
sub-team, 123–124
technical project management, 89
technological savvy, 86–87
timeboxed schedules, definition, 123
volunteer
  cultivating, 120–121
  non-performing, 107
  reassigning, 119–120
  recruiting, 109–113, 115–117
volunteer engagement, 132
volunteer information form, 111f–112f
volunteerism, changes in, 9–10
volunteer job, defining, 117
volunteer-managed project, case study, 121–125
volunteer position description, example, 101f
volunteers
  and expectations, 106
  identifying needs, 99–102
  managing, 99–108, 115–121
  overseeing, 106–107
  in resource pool, 24–26
  responsibilities of, 24–26
  retaining, 113–114
  turnover, 106
WBS, *see* work breakdown structure
weighted average, definition, 52
work breakdown structure (WBS)
  definition, 34
  developing, 46–49
  example, 47f
work packages, definition, 52

ABOUT THE AUTHORS

Karen R. J. White, PMP, PMI Fellow, is the founder of Applied Agility, an organization focused on helping nonprofits achieve success with their strategic objectives. She has managed numerous projects for small and large nonprofits, ranging in diversity from the Girl Scouts to healthcare centers to international museums to universities.

Karen was formerly a senior consultant and director with PM Solutions, where she assisted many Fortune 500 firms in implementing project management best practices. She has served as a board director for the Project Management Institute as well as Chair of the PMI Educational Foundation. In 2009 she was named a PMI Fellow.

Karen is recognized internationally for her leadership in the profession and as a thought leader in the practice of agile project management. She is the author of *Agile Project Management: A Mandate for the 21st Century* (Center for Business Practices, 2009) and contributed to *The AMA Handbook of Project Management* (AMACOM, 2010) and *Project Management Maturity Model* (Auerbach Publications, 2006). Karen holds an MS in Information Systems from Northeastern University.

Pamela Puleo, FAHP, CFRE, is vice president for community affairs at Concord Hospital in New Hampshire and oversees a division that includes Volunteer Services, Hospitality Services, Public Affairs, Marketing, the gift shop, and the cancer boutique. She also serves as a member of the hospital's senior management team. Since 2007 she has also served as the executive director for the Concord Hospital Trust, which serves as the hospital's philanthropic arm.

Having achieved the highest level of certification available in the field of healthcare philanthropy (Fellow of the Association for Healthcare Philanthropy), she has nearly thirty years of experience in philanthropy, volunteer management, and public relations for not-for-profit organizations, nine of which were with the American Cancer Society in three New England States and twenty three with Concord Hospital.

Pamela has served as a board member for CONFR (Council on Fundraising), board member and president for the New England Association for Healthcare Philanthropy, and board member for the Association for Healthcare Philanthropy (AHP), including terms as the treasurer, vice chair for education and certification, and vice chair for membership and communications. In addition she has served on numerous community boards and committees in New Hampshire, including Special Olympics, United Way Allocations Committee, Merrimack-Concord SPCA, CATCH Neighborhood Housing, and Early Learning New Hampshire.